Paradise

for Sale

FLORIDA'S BOOMS AND BUSTS

NICK WYNNE & RICHARD MOORHEAD

Charleston — London

THE
History
PRESS

Published by The History Press
Charleston, SC 29403
www.historypress.net

Copyright © 2010 by Nick Wynne and Richard Moorhead
All rights reserved

First published 2010

Manufactured in the United States

ISBN 978.1.59629.844.6

Library of Congress Cataloging-in-Publication Data

Wynne, Nick.
Paradise for sale : Florida's booms and busts / Nick Wynne and Richard Moorhead.
p. cm.
ISBN 978-1-59629-844-6
1. Florida--History, Local. 2. Florida--Biography. 3. Real estate development--
Florida--History. I. Moorhead, Richard, 1943- II. Title.
F311.W96 2010
975.9--dc22
2009050442

For Debra and Lisa Wynne

For Sandy Moorhead

Contents

Acknowledgements

A ny author knows that there are people who provide tremendous insights and assistance on any writing project. It certainly is true in this instance. We are deeply indebted to Sandy Moorhead, Debra Wynne, June Geiger, Peggy Ryals, George "Speedy" Harrell, Jack Rabun, Ada E. Parrish and the staff and volunteers of the Florida Historical Society Library in Cocoa for helping us run down pictures and books. We are also grateful for the "laying on of hands" that they occasionally performed on the manuscript.

We are especially grateful for the many authors who have written on this topic in the past and for their research.

Introduction

S tealing from one writer," Wilson Mizner is reputed to have said, "is plagiarism. Stealing from many is research." If that is true, this book is well researched. The story of Florida's boom and subsequent bust of the 1920s is a story that has been told often and exceedingly well, but with the exception of David Nolan's *Fifty Feet in Paradise*, it is a story that has been told in pieces. We hope this book will help consolidate the story even more.

The first impression a listener or reader gets when discovering the boom is that it lasted for many years, but that is not the case. The boom was a short-lived affair, lasting barely twenty-four or so months at its height, but it took two years (1921–23) to get started and another two years (1927–28) to die. However, the years 1925 and 1926 were glorious years, unrivaled in American history, when millions of dollars were tossed around like so much confetti. Far outstripping the fabulous gold and silver rushes of the 1800s and early 1900s in monetary value, the Florida land boom made overnight millionaires a common occurrence and rags-to-riches tales a dime a dozen.

Virtually every part of the Sunshine State had a leading "boomer" who was responsible for focusing attention on his particular section—Addison Mizner in Palm Beach and Boca Raton, Carl Fisher in Miami Beach, George Merrick in Coral Gables, David P. "Doc" Davis in Tampa and St. Augustine, John Ringling in Sarasota and Barron Collier in southwest Florida. For every giant in the public eye, there were scores of other, lesser-known figures who duplicated their efforts on a smaller scale—Carl Dann Sr. in Orlando, D.

Collins Gillette in Temple Terrace, Walter Fuller in St. Petersburg, William J. Howey in Lake County and the list goes on and on.

Everyone in Florida benefitted from the boom. The price of the average home, away from the hubbub of development communities, rose by a remarkable 200 percent, a feat that remained unsurpassed until the real estate explosion of 2005–06. Jobs were plentiful—so much so that northern contractors brought workers with them, and inmates in Florida jails worked grading streets, unloading ships and completing construction of needed infrastructure. Banks, long distrusted and few in number in 1920, suddenly began to spring up overnight and reported millions of dollars in deposits. Credit was easy to come by, and money poured into the Sunshine State in torrents. Chain banking, a new innovation, gave access to the deposits of northern banks and banks in other southern states. It seemed that only the most slothful could fail to get his fair share.

People came to Florida by trains, steamships and automobiles. The Model-T Ford became the icon of the period, signifying a major shift in societal dynamics as mobility and freedom replaced stability and tedium. Prohibition, the Jazz Age, gambling, the rise of the middle class, wild stories of fortunes made in minutes and an atmosphere of constant happenings were all disparate elements that cooked in the cauldron that was boom Florida. Greats, near greats, the famous, the infamous, movie stars, politicians, athletes, ne'er-do-wells, preachers, foreign royalty, con artists, educators, labor leaders, union members—every element of American and world society showed up in the Sunshine State. It was a gigantic party. Florida was a perpetual motion machine—destined to go on forever.

The party and the perpetual motion machine came to a screeching halt in 1927. The Sunshine State, which had offered so much promise just a year earlier, entered the doldrums. For almost two decades, it remained there—baking in the hot sun, scarred by empty subdivisions, decorative arches over roads that led to nowhere and languishing amidst fields of broken promises.

In the years that followed the 1920s, Floridians eagerly sought to reclaim the halcyon days of that decade and every little surge in the state's economy quickly became a "boom." It is still true today—boom, boomlet, bust—all part of the lexicon of Floridians, and all very real parts of the Florida economy. Nevertheless, hope springs eternal!

CHAPTER 1

An American Eden

Oldest of all [states] *in its history, it is the youngest of all in its development. But as the acts of Florida's unmatchable climate, its unrivalled agricultural and horticultural possibilities and its limitless opportunities in commerce and industry become known of all men, it cannot fail to become one of the richest, most populous and influential in the whole family of commonwealths which make up our Nation. The sun of Florida's destiny has risen, and only the malicious and the short-sighted contend or believe it will ever set.*
—*Governor John W. Martin, Foreword,* Florida in the Making, *1926*

From the earliest days of European settlement, Florida has been a business venture. Pedro Menéndez de Avilés, the explorer and colonizer who planted the Spanish flag and established St. Augustine, referred to it as "the enterprise of Florida." And what an enterprise it has been for the past five hundred years! Juan Ponce de León, the discoverer of Florida, has entered popular legend as seeking a "fountain of youth" that would give those who drank from it eternal life and perpetual youth—a myth that is not backed by facts, but one that endures nevertheless. Ponce de León's legend set the standard for many of those who came after him, and myths became an integral part of most promotional campaigns. The wilds of the Florida peninsula—the peninsula was not completely surveyed until the early nineteenth century—held the prospect of always being something more than reality, and the mystery of the unexplored merely fueled the imaginations of those willing to be misled.

With its acquisition by the United States in 1821, promoters launched a multitude of advertising campaigns to bring settlers and tourists into Florida. There was little to recommend Florida to the American public—three hundred years of occupation by the Spanish and the British had barely pushed the frontier much beyond a line about thirty miles from the coasts of the Atlantic Ocean and the Gulf of Mexico. Pensacola and St. Augustine—and to a lesser extent, Fernandina—were the only towns of note, and these were barely larger than many New England villages. The isolation of Americans in Florida changed rapidly, however, as scions of established planting families in the mid- and upper South hurried to claim large blocks of land in North Florida and to use the slaves they brought with them to establish a plantation culture based on the cultivation of cotton and tobacco. By the time Florida became a state in 1845, planters controlled the financial, social and political affairs of the Sunshine State.

When the call came to secede from the Union in 1860–61, Floridians hastily joined their kinfolk in the other Southern states and cast aside statehood after a brief sixteen years. During the Civil War, thousands of Floridians served on battlefields far removed from their homes. Unable to defend all of Florida, Confederate officials were content to allow Union forces to occupy both coasts and Key West. Only one major battle, Olustee, was fought in Florida, and although that battle resulted in an overwhelming Confederate victory, it did little to halt the continued Union presence in the state.

Union soldiers in Florida were impressed with what they found. Mostly sunny tropical weather made their service in the state pleasant, while the few colder days of winter were mild when compared to the harsh winters in the North. Tropical foliage, citrus trees that grew with wild abandon and abundant wildlife—to say nothing of the vast tracts of open land—convinced most of these occupying troops that Florida was as close to paradise as any place in the world. The Florida they experienced left vivid memories that drew them back to this "Eden."

When the war ended in 1865, Florida experienced a minor population boom. Wealthy planters no longer controlled every aspect of life in the Sunshine State, which left the state open to development by aggressive entrepreneurs and determined farmers. The previously unexplored and largely unsettled lands south of St. Augustine and Ocala, the domain of a relative few cow men before the war, now became a magnet to draw the lower classes from northern cities, as well as disgruntled ex-Confederates eager to suffer the agony of defeat in quiet isolation. Like the vast prairies of the

Midwest, Florida offered these individuals a chance to create a new society away from the domination of aristocratic families and factory bosses.

With little in the way of manufacturing concerns and few mineral resources, early efforts to "sell" Florida centered on the natural resources of the state. Abundant wildlife, a balmy climate and the prospect of producing large and profitable crops featured prominently in the millions of pamphlets and brochures sent out by agricultural associations, land developers and government agencies. So, too, did the plethora of postcards and broadsides produced by the owners of small hotels that lined the rivers of the state. Florida, potential visitors and settlers were informed, was a land that was so fertile that seeds spilled on the ground germinated and produced bumper crops. In fact, so the popular legends went, it was possible to simply come to Florida, construct a rudimentary home and live off the widely available fruits that proliferated endlessly under the nourishing sunshine that bathed the state every day. In practically every area of the state during the late 1800s, utopian dreamers bought land for as little as fifty cents an acre and built communities for those who shared their visions. Although most realized within a few months that a life of ease with little labor was a pipe dream, Florida lost little of its initial appeal, and those who came to farm the land generally stayed. A larger group of individuals who responded to these advertisements realized that the key to success in the Sunshine State was to take advantage of the cheap land prices and work hard.

Hotel owners stressed the flora and fauna that made Florida an exotic wonderland. Visitors who usually came for a two- or three-month stay could fish the unlimited and unpolluted lakes, lagoons and rivers and, for more excitement, hunt the hammocks that abounded on the peninsula. The absence of seasonal restrictions or limits on kills invited them to engage in an orgy of hunting. Even a few of the more daring sought out the dangerous alligators that lurked at the edges of the myriad bodies of fresh water.

Florida was marketed as a healthy refuge for those who suffered from arthritis, myalgia and other assorted ills. The perpetually warm climate also lured individuals who suffered from respiratory diseases like croup, asthma and consumption. Across the Sunshine State, small sanatoriums and spas sprang up around the fresh springs that abounded. Many who came stayed after their diseases had gone into remission or went back home to preach the healing virtues of Florida's climate.

Despite a continuous stream of propaganda leaflets that flooded the other states, the actual number of permanent new residents to Florida remained

Prior to the 1920s, the majority of hotels in Florida were usually wooden structures with twenty-five to forty rooms that offered visitors the opportunity to hunt, fish and enjoy nature. This photograph of the Rockledge House Hotel (circa 1895) was typical. Note the young woman with the shotgun standing in front of the steps. *Courtesy of the Florida Historical Society.*

Henry Plant's Tampa Bay Hotel cost $3 million to build and contained furnishings purchased in Europe for more than $1 million. The grounds of the hotel featured a nine-hole golf course, hunting grounds, a casino and wildlife such as deer and turkeys—all just a stone's throw across the narrow Hillsboro River from the city of Tampa. *Courtesy of the Moorhead Collection.*

low. The absence of passable roads and the necessity to remain close to rivers made settlement difficult; that is, until the 1880s. During that decade, entrepreneurs Henry Flagler and Henry Plant reinvigorated the push for new settlers when they drove railroad lines down the east and west coasts. For the first time, vast new areas opened to settlement. Plant and Flagler sought to bolster the success of their lines by erecting large resort hotels that offered visitors a chance to experience the wilderness of the Sunshine State without giving up any of the luxuries of older, more established resorts. The railroad companies created departments within their corporate structures that had the sole purpose of enticing Americans to come to Florida. The coffers of the railroads and their hotels depended on how well these departments did the job, and both Plant and Flagler hired the best persons for the job. Organized sports—golf, sailing, polo—became the linchpin of the advertising campaigns for the resorts, and although many of the ads showed great expanses of beaches, practically none actually touted them as places to have fun. That would come later.

Of course, smaller hotels, owned by independents, benefited from the buzz created by the railroads. Piggybacking on the lavish advertisements of the corporate giants, they generated their own ads. It was practically impossible to pick up a newspaper north of the Mason-Dixon line without being assaulted by a multiplicity of ads for Florida hotels, urban developments and productive farmlands.

Very quickly, however, the railroads realized that the income generated by passengers and by hotel guests would not be sufficient to pay the operating costs of the roads nor to produce a profit for shareholders. To be successful, the roads had to find customers for the large tracts of land awarded by the state for each mile of railroad construction. Much as the railroads had done in the American West, the corporations formed land companies to market the raw acreage they owned. Because much of their holdings were located in rural areas, railroad companies stressed the desirability of owning a farm in this modern Garden of Eden. Testimonials from prominent public figures and satisfied owners filled the advertising brochures mailed to millions of Americans. Civic organizations, financial advisors, churches and virtually any other recognized group with a mailing address repeatedly received mass mailings about the wonders of Florida. Local boards of trade extolled the economic benefits of Florida, but these brochures, usually filled to overflowing with dry facts on farm production, transportation and land costs, were difficult reading. Nevertheless, they contributed to the massive effort to sell the Sunshine State.

Hotelier and railroad magnate Henry Plant loved the game of golf and frequently played it with guests of his hotels. Notice the formal dress of the individual players. *Courtesy of the Moorhead Collection.*

Once again, smaller landowners tied on to the campaigns of the railroads, and the Florida "land boom," which would last until the 1920s, was underway. Businessmen and governmental departments combined as chambers of commerce to promote the state, while professional associations of farmers cooperated with the promotional efforts by utilizing brightly colored labels on their products that also stressed only positive aspects of the Florida experience. Oranges, celery, corn and pineapples received their share of the limelight, and potential farm buyers were assured that with just a little work they could be successful.

Certainly, Florida had its share of individuals and entrepreneurs seeking to mine the bright sunshine and open spaces of the Sunshine State and to convert them into hard cash. Like some exotic El Dorado, Florida beckoned adventuresome rogues and visionaries to its shores, and many came with schemes that they thought would make them fortunes overnight. While some of these individuals were earnest and honest, some were less worried about morals and more concerned with making a dollar. Because of actions by less scrupulous promoters, "buying Florida land" became the accepted equivalent of "purchasing the Brooklyn Bridge," but even this new addition to the American lexicon did little to hurt their marketing success. Only later, when the United States experienced the Great Depression, was the full impact of this humorous warning appreciated.

By the beginning of the twentieth century, technological innovations combined to make the marketing of Florida a resounding success. Photography, which had evolved from the cumbersome process of glass negatives and static subjects, now offered quick processing and the ability to take action photographs. Hand painting also brought a sense of excitement to the products of the photographers' eyes. In addition, photographers had pioneered ways in which photographs could be "doctored" to remove unwanted objects or to add new features. Fully adhering to the adage that "a picture is worth a thousand words," these modern-day Rembrandts set about to create idyllic pictures of a Florida with clear blue skies, azure water, pristine beaches and lush tropical landscapes. Professional public relations firms in large metropolitan areas produced effective advertisements, and scores of local imitators copied their style and churned out their own versions of these ads.

New developments in printing made it possible to reproduce these colored images by the millions, along with the bright, eye-catching graphics generated by thousands of commercial artists. Utilizing the new schools of art nouveau and art deco design, they produced countless brochures, maps, postcards, labels and letterheads that featured idealized landscapes, resort hotels, farms and housing developments. These materials reminded recipients that Florida was beautiful, fun, affordable and the destination of choice of millions of "in" people. Hyperbole ruled the day, and the general operating principle of ad writers was to exaggerate the positive and ignore the negative. As the twentieth century progressed, depictions of bathing beauties, golfers in their knickers and visitors exploring under a cloudless sky reinforced these elements. If these ads were the only available source of information about the Sunshine State, the reader would be forced to believe that it never rained in Florida, that every person in the state wore a perpetual smile and that orange trees and palm trees lined every road and filled every yard. A leading newspaper, the *St. Petersburg Evening Independent*, went so far as to promise a free newspaper to every subscriber on the days it rained.

The rapid adoption of the automobile as the primary mode of travel in the United States by the 1920s also accelerated the merchandising of the Sunshine State. The need for maps and the rise of tourist attractions such as Bok Tower, Silver Springs and McKee Gardens provided new fodder

By the 1920s, the widespread use of color in advertising brochures had attracted the attention of tourists and potential home buyers to the wonders of Florida. The use of bathing beauties in scanty (for the period) swimsuits offered hints of exotic adventures. *Courtesy of the Florida Historical Society.*

for new ads. Hundreds of mom and pop roadside motels and fruit stands were opened to take advantage of the new automobile tourists, who left the well-known paths along rivers and railroads to head into the interior of the peninsula. Once again, the local entrepreneurs found that the professionally produced advertisements of the larger resorts could be modified cheaply and easily to fit their businesses.

Automobiles not only increased the number of tourists in Florida, but their ability to traverse the entirety of the peninsula also spurred the development of an aggressive and nonstop building boom in the early 1920s. Across the Florida landscape, individuals like George Merrick, D.P. "Doc" Davis, Carl Fisher and numerous other smaller developers bought large parcels of land and subdivided them into smaller parcels for homes. Deliberately drawing a comparison with the sunny climate of the Mediterranean, these developers hired nationally known architects to recreate the tiled roofs, archways and patios of Spanish and Italian villas in Miami, Boca Raton, Vero Beach and Tampa. Some developers, like Addison Mizner, designed their own homes without the benefit of formal training as architects. What was popular in the larger cities soon found its way to the smaller towns and villages. Only the North Florida cities of Jacksonville and Tallahassee appeared to escape this mania for the Mediterranean, and perhaps that was because they were geographically more identified with the Old South states of Georgia and Alabama than they were with lower Florida.

Although the boom of the early 1920s came to a screeching halt in 1926–27, the collapse of the era of rapid building was neither absolute nor permanent. Even as the rest of America settled into a severe depression after the stock market crash of 1929, many of America's wealthiest families and a significant number of the middle class managed to weather the crash with most, if not all, of their assets in place. The distress of small farmers and small businessmen had little effect on their incomes. Throughout the 1930s, a few Florida developers continued to build hotels and large homes for these elites. Miami Beach, which has seen a revival in its economic fortunes during the last two decades, continued to be a favorite watering hole for them. South Beach's famous art deco and art moderne hotels were constructed during the Depression, and hoteliers had little difficulty in keeping their rooms filled.

Even in the depths of the Depression, Floridians believed that the cure for whatever economic woes the state faced could be solved by ratcheting up their advertising efforts. If advertising selling the Sunshine State worked in good times, they reasoned, more of it should work in hard times. To a certain extent, this reasoning was correct. Large cities, already known for their playground atmospheres and whose names carried a certain social imprimatur, did survive and even mildly prospered. Smaller cities were less fortunate and weathered the Depression at a subsistence level. Small developers like Cocoa Beach's Gus Edwards were forced to put their plans on hold to await better economic conditions. Even through this wait, prolonged by the outbreak of World War II, their plans continued to percolate on the back burner. In Edwards's case, his grandiose plans for Cocoa Beach did not come to fruition until the late 1950s and the advent of the space race. Today, the observant traveler in Florida's backcountry areas can find entire towns with streets paved and utilities in place but no houses. Some are the products of the '20s bust, while others were built during the anticipated boom of the 1950s. Most are out of the way, with little in the way of amenities to attract settlers, and many are tied up in court battles that seem to drag on endlessly.

From its earliest days as a Spanish colony through the present, Florida has attracted the attention of many people, and much of this attention has been generated through the creation and distribution of advertisements tailored to selling the possibilities of the peninsula. The success of these efforts can readily be seen by the astronomical growth of the state's population. From a mere 1.5 million permanent residents in 1950, Florida now has more than 18.5 million citizens. Despite a growing shortage of potable water and a rapidly declining amount of buildable acreage, the "selling" machines of Florida have been in existence for so long that no one knows how to stop them. Politicians who depend on continued growth as a mark of good leadership have little or no interest in developing a rational alternative to continued unregulated growth.

Today, more than 85 million tourists visit the Sunshine State each year, brought here by advertisements placed in every possible media outlet. Governments at all levels—state, county and municipal—annually spend millions of dollars to increase the number of visitors. Each of Florida's sixty-seven counties has a tourist development board with special taxing powers that generate the dollars spent to extol the opportunities of that county. No citizen is even surprised when tourist officials make trips to Europe and the Far East to recruit more visitors. Neither are they surprised when government leaders offer tax exemptions and free land to companies willing to locate in the Sunshine State.

It was all about selling, and success is all about numbers.

CHAPTER 2

Priming the Pump

Lotus land invaded by reality and still retaining its languorous atmosphere—that's Florida…Florida represents the fruition of America's dream for a playground.
—William Ullman, American Motorist, *October 1926*

When the twentieth century dawned, Florida was enjoying a mini-boom in land purchases. Caught up in the fervor of the Plant-Flagler railroad expansion of the previous two decades and the rise of resort hotels that catered to the super-rich, investors—attracted by the prospect of so much money in so few cities—flocked to places like Miami, Jacksonville, Tampa and Palm Beach. Other investors, seeing the possibilities of great financial returns for farming and industrial ventures, purchased huge swaths of Florida lands and experimented with a variety of truck crops, mining operations and utopian communities. Here and there, in places like Miami and Sarasota, other entrepreneurs platted their holdings and offered homesteads for sale. Almost exclusively, however, the emphasis was placed on attracting wealthy buyers, who would spend a few winter months each year enjoying the sunshine, playing a few rounds of golf or games of tennis, bathing in community pools and taking in the natural flora and fauna that abounded in Florida.

In Palm Beach, for example, wealthy visitors who arrived in private railway cars or by luxurious yachts stayed at Flagler's luxury hotels, where, surrounded by the "right kind" of people, they could flagrantly display their wealth and compare net worth with one another. Unlike Newport, Rhode

Island, where large mansions were built as summer homes for the ultra-wealthy of the nineteenth century, Palm Beach was a "hotel civilization," which served as an outpost for the nation's richest families, Ward McAllister's "Four Hundred." Flagler's aim was to provide all of the possible recreation activities a guest could ever want within the boundaries of the hotel property. Days were spent fishing, cycling, golfing and playing tennis and croquet, while men and women both frequently practiced their marksmanship on the various sea birds that filled the sky. Tame pigeons, freed from their cages, presented predictable targets for avid shooters during organized "hunts." Despite the variety of activities available to the more active visitors, David Paul "Doc" Davis, who gained fame as the developer of Davis Islands in Tampa during the early 1920s, referred to the Palm Beach lifestyle as sedentary and for old people. His assessment was right on target, simply because many of the fortunes on exhibit in Palm Beach had taken decades to establish.

Initially, Palm Beach, unlike Newport, was open to anyone who could afford the high prices charged for extended stays at the Breakers or the Royal Poinciana hotels. Money—or as one resident wag described it, "filthy lucre"—became the standard for acceptance, and America's nouveau riche rubbed shoulders with scions of long-established wealth and even European royalty. During the first decade of the twentieth century, many of America's patent medicine kings found Palm Beach a delightful place to vacation with their families. Alva Johnston, in his book *The Legendary Mizners*, described how various individuals were referred to by the source of their wealth instead of their given names. Thus, Isaac Emerson, whose Bromo-Seltzer factory in Baltimore produced the "morning after" favorite of inebriates, was most often referred to as "Bromo-Seltzer" Emerson, while Dr. Jonas Kilmer of Binghamton, New York, was popularly called "Swamp Root" after his famous elixir. Truly, Palm Beach operated as a democracy of wealth, a standard that adheres today when such newly rich persons as Donald Trump and Rush Limbaugh can purchase homes there and attain status as members of the social elite.

In 1896, Henry Flagler extended his railroad, now named the Florida East Coast Railway, to Miami. Devastating freezes in the winter of 1894–95 in Palm Beach caused him to look farther south. Offers of free land from Julia Tuttle and the William Brickell family enticed him to come to Miami, an offer he accepted and which paid untold dividends to the donors. With his arrival in the city, Flagler wasted little time in duplicating the strategy that had proven so profitable in the past. Within

Henry Morrison Flagler, a Standard Oil partner of John D. Rockefeller, visited St. Augustine in 1881 and became enchanted with the prospects of making money on Florida tourism, land sales and his railroad. In 1885, he started construction on the Ponce de León Hotel in the city. By 1896, his enterprises stretched as far south as Miami, and by 1912, Key West, then the largest city in Florida, was connected to the mainland by Flagler rails. *Courtesy of the Florida Historical Society.*

a few months, he undertook civic improvements, including dredging a channel to open Biscayne Bay to shipping, building the first water and power systems in the area, constructing streets where none had existed before and starting the city's first newspaper, the *Miami Metropolis*. Flagler's arrival turned a small village into a viable town, and though gratified at the offer, he refused to have the town named in his honor when it was incorporated in 1896. In 1897, he opened the exclusive Royal Palm Hotel, which stretched 680 feet along the shore of the Miami River and featured a number of firsts for the city—the first electric lights, the first elevator and the first swimming pool.

Without a doubt, Flagler put Miami on the map. Prior to the coming of the railroad, there was little about it to merit even the distinction of being a village. By 1905, however, Flagler turned his attention southward once again. He set his sights on Key West, the southernmost city in the United States and, at that time, the most populated city in Florida. Accessible only by boat, Key West was connected to Florida by a chain of small cays that stretched 128 miles long and was located in the heart of the hurricane zone.

By 1900, however, the mere presence of the railroad magnate and hotelier had attracted considerable interest from some of the more established and wealthier citizens of the United States. William Deering, the chairman of the Deering Harvester Company, and his wife, Clara, built a large home in the Coconut Grove section of south Miami. He was soon joined by other members of America's financial and social elite, and Mary Brickell, now the widow of William Brickell, sold lots to them. Luxurious mansions soon lined Miami's "Millionaire's Row," a visible display of how attractive the town had become.

Deering's two sons, James and Charles, soon followed suit and purchased land for homes. James Deering constructed Villa Vizcaya, a massive thirty-four-room Italian Renaissance villa, designed by F. Burrall Hoffman Jr. and Phineas E. Paist (and decorated by Paul Chalfin), encompassing 180 acres, complete with formal gardens, statuary, a small complementary village and fields for grazing livestock and growing produce. Chalfin and Deering toured Europe to purchase furnishings and antiques for the mansion. By 1922, the mansion was complete—and all for the equivalent of $60 million in today's dollars.

Charles Deering, who became the first chairman of the International Harvester Company when Deering Harvester merged with McCormick Harvester Company in 1902, was an avid naturalist and art patron. His 444-acre estate, which initially incorporated the older Richmond Inn as the

Villa Vizcaya, built by James Deering, sat on 180 acres of prime Miami real estate. Built for an estimated $60 million in today's dollars, this opulent mansion and its bachelor owner hosted a number of prominent celebrities when it was completed in 1922. *Courtesy of the Florida Historical Society.*

principal residence but later included the Stone House (built in 1922), was larger than Vizcaya but never as opulent. Both brothers were art collectors whose massive collections were worth millions at their deaths.

The Deering family was the most prominent of the wealthy northerners to build in Miami before World War I, but they were not the only family to do so. A small but thriving real estate business added to the prosperity of the city as more and more moneyed individuals built winter homes there.

Slightly north of downtown Miami, John Collins, an agricultural pioneer, owned a large mangrove island where he managed to grow a considerable crop of avocados. In 1913, unable to depend on boats to take his crop to waiting ships in Biscayne Bay, he began construction of a narrow wooden bridge to connect his island to the mainland. When the bridge was about three-quarters finished, Collins ran out of money. Carl Fisher, who was visiting the city on his much-delayed honeymoon flush with $5 million he had recently gotten from the sale of his famous Prest-O-Lite company, which manufactured gas-powered headlights for automobiles, somehow met him (the stories of how the meeting came about vary from source to source) and advanced him $50,000 to complete the bridge. In exchange, Fisher received a one-mile-long strip of land, six hundred yards wide, that fronted on the Atlantic Ocean. He also purchased additional acreage immediately behind the frontage parcels.

The Collins Bridge, completed with a $50,000 loan from Carl Fisher, opened a mangrove island to development. With Fisher's vision and money, this island eventually became the posh resort of Miami Beach. *Courtesy of the Florida Historical Society.*

Carl Fisher, an entrepreneur from Indianapolis, spent millions of dollars to pump ocean sand onto a mangrove island to create Miami Beach, where he wanted to develop an American Riviera. *Courtesy of the Historical Association of Southern Florida.*

Priming the Pump

Dredging sand from the bottom of the ocean, Fisher widened his holdings on Miami Beach and created several artificial islands for additional homesites. *Courtesy of the Florida Historical Society.*

Fisher, who would become synonymous in later years with the city of Miami Beach, was an unlikely investor. Long associated with the automobile industry, he had manufactured Empire cars and pioneered the use of gas-powered headlights, was a leading figure in the movement to build cross-country highways and, most notably, was the major force behind the construction of the Indianapolis Motor Speedway. Fisher immediately announced that he would invest $5 million to create a new Palm Beach, which he named Miami Beach. To this end, he hired dredges to pump sand from the ocean floor—twenty-four hours a day—onto the mangroves to create new land. After pumping more than six million tons of sand and spending hundreds of thousands of dollars to remove the persistent mangrove stumps, he began to lay out his new city. Quickly, other property owners followed suit.

Derided by Miami real estate promoters, Fisher nevertheless proceeded to clear land, build infrastructure, lay out polo fields and yacht clubs and build a small thirty-two-room hotel, the Lincoln. His objective, he stated to one and all, was to create an American Riviera where wealthy Americans could find all of the attractions and amenities offered by any European resort. Although the United States was initially neutral in the conflict, World War I, which began in 1914 and soon involved most European countries and their colonies, seemed tailor-made to boost Fisher's plans, since submarine warfare

Although he started this project prior to World War I, Fisher's Miami Beach resort did not become a reality until the 1920s. His first hotel, built in 1916 and named in honor of President Abraham Lincoln, was a modest building of only thirty-two rooms. *Courtesy of the Historical Association of Southern Florida.*

made steamship crossings of the Atlantic Ocean difficult at best. The sinking of the *Lusitania* in 1915 and the horrific violence of the land war ended the practice of leisurely boarding a steamship, cruising across the ocean for a week to ten days, meandering from capital to capital, visiting historical sites and museums and spending weeks on end at various resorts and spas. While a few intrepid younger persons braved the danger of an ocean voyage, most Americans stayed home. These people made up the market to whom Fisher wanted to sell his land.

Prior to his arrival in Miami, Fisher had been one of the movers and shakers in the effort to build a cross-continent highway to stimulate the automobile industry, since he was a partner in the Empire Automobile Company, an Indiana concern that produced a family car to compete with the cars manufactured by Henry Ford and others in Detroit. Although successful in raising a considerable amount of money and generating the support of communities across the United States, the highway was unfinished when the United States entered World War I. When he acquired land in the Miami area, he also began promoting a major north–south highway that would run from Michigan to Miami. His interest in highway construction coincided with the emerging "Good Roads" movement in the United States and his desire to promote his automotive and development businesses.

Priming the Pump

Although he enjoyed some small success in selling land prior to the end of the war, Fisher did not sell enough to recoup his investment. However, the pump was primed.

Southwest of Miami, another visionary, George Edgar Merrick, was also priming the pump for future development. His father, a well-educated though sickly minister, had purchased a small 160-acre family farm in 1898. The farm, which was called Coral Gables Plantation, produced vegetables for the growing market in Miami and seedlings for the burgeoning citrus market. The venture was profitable enough that George, the eldest child, was sent to Rollins College, although he had never acquired a high school diploma. At Rollins, he did exceptionally well and soon left to study at Columbia University. His academic career was cut short, however, when his father died in 1911 and George returned to manage the family's holdings. Before his death, Solomon Merrick, George's father, attempted to attract well-educated and learned friends to the Coral Gables area in an attempt to found a community of scholars. Although only a few friends took him up on the idea, the concept of developing a self-contained community did not die. After he took over the reins of Coral Gables Plantation, George Merrick adopted his father's vision, but with major changes. Influenced by the City Beautiful movement that swept America following the 1893 Columbian Exposition, the younger Merrick began to entertain the idea of an entirely new city, which would incorporate the latest concepts of city planning and architectural controls. His new bride, Eunice Peacock, whom he married in 1916, shared his vision, but when he approached area bankers about financing to buy additional land, they arbitrarily dismissed him because his proposed new city had no waterfront property and was several miles from Biscayne Bay.

Momentarily frustrated, the Merricks persisted in their dream. George took a job as a real estate salesman and used his earnings to increase the size of his holdings. By 1919, he had amassed more than sixteen hundred acres that would become the core of his proposed new city in the years that followed. Unlike Fisher, whose Miami Beach was designed to cater to the wealthiest Americans during the winter months, Merrick's Coral Gables aimed for year-round middle-class residents, whose investments would provide them with permanent residences. In his vision of the perfect city, citizens would be able to take advantage of the sunshine and activities twelve months each year. It was a dream whose time was yet to come.

In Sarasota, fifty miles south of Tampa, Bertha Palmer, the widow of hotelier and real estate baron Potter Palmer of Chicago, arrived in 1902

George Edgar Merrick, using the family's 160-acre plantation as the core of his holdings, gradually acquired more than 1,600 acres to the west of Miami. Influenced by the City Beautiful movement of the early 1900s, he created Coral Gables, a new city with planned streets, family homes and civic attractions—all regulated by rigid zoning restrictions. This is the original family home in Coral Gables. *Courtesy of the Historical Association of Southern Florida.*

to survey property in the area. A small advertisement in the *Chicago Sunday Tribune* offered large tracts of land "suitable for citrus growing" around Sarasota by Joseph H. Lord and Arthur B. Edwards. Intrigued, she got in touch with Lord, made arrangements to go to Sarasota and eventually wound up purchasing some 140,000 acres of Florida land. Mrs. Palmer utilized some of her vast holdings to grow citrus, which proved very profitable for her, and some to raise cattle, which were hybrids between the descendants of small, wiry Spanish cows and Brahma bulls. Some 7,000 acres were dedicated to Bee Ridge, which was to be a model farm development of 10- to 40-acre farms. This project ended in failure when some early purchasers became dissatisfied and gave up their land, and many of the remaining parcels went unsold. In 1914, on the outskirts of Tampa, Mrs. Palmer purchased a large tract of citrus groves and wild land for use as a hunting preserve—land that would ultimately become the boom-era Temple Terrace development.

She devoted other sections of land to development and resale through her firm, the Sarasota-Venice Company. In 1916, Palmer invited a New York

Left: Bertha Palmer, the eccentric and rich widow of Potter Palmer of Chicago, was attracted to the Sarasota area by an ad in the *Chicago Sunday Tribune*. When she arrived in 1902, she began to buy up available land. By the time of her death in 1918, she owned more than 140,000 acres. *Courtesy of the Florida Historical Society*.

Below: When Bertha Palmer owned Temple Terrace, the family used it for hunting and for growing oranges, but after Maude Fowler and Collins Gillett purchased the property in the early 1920s, it became an exclusive golf community. *Courtesy of the Tampa-Hillsborough County Public Library System*.

firm to develop a plan to make Venice into a "Palm Beach West," which would feature golfing, hunting, fishing and other activities. She quickly lost interest in the project when the planners asked her to set aside a sizeable portion of her most valuable property for the construction of public-use buildings. Her plans for further development were put on hold when, that same year, she discovered she had incurable cancer. Her death in 1918 ended her schemes. She had profited from her investments in the Sunshine State, however, and the executors for her estate estimated that she had grown her fortune from the $8 million she had inherited from her late husband into almost $20 million, with most of the growth coming from her dealings in Florida land. Although Bertha Palmer was dead before the great boom of the 1920s, she had primed the pump by demonstrating that Florida lands, when purchased at a fair price and developed intelligently, would return considerable profits.

Palmer's efforts to develop Sarasota and the surrounding region attracted the attention of other wealthy individuals. In 1911, John Ringling, the great American circus entrepreneur, came to Sarasota. He was so impressed with the prospects for potential development that he persuaded his brother Charles to join him the next year. Soon, John Ringling was joined by other family members who shared his enthusiasm for the area. He amassed more than sixty thousand acres by 1917, including several of the small islands that buffered the city from the Gulf of Mexico. Although the attention of most Americans was directed toward the war in Europe, which the United States had joined that year, John Ringling was poised to take the maximum advantage of his investment when peace returned. Once he had decided to put roots down in Sarasota, Ringling and his wife, Mabel, launched a major project to build a mansion suitable for persons of their wealth.

The efforts of these large prewar developers did not go unnoticed in Florida or the rest of the nation. In many of the smaller towns of the state, men with lesser fortunes began to piece together parcels of land and to plat them into subdivisions. Some, like Cocoa city attorney Gus Edwards, formed a small syndicate of local residents to purchase six hundred acres on the barrier island where present-day Cocoa Beach is located. In central Florida, Charles Hosmer Morse, a wealthy Chicago businessman, purchased a large tract of land in the mid-1890s, when successive freezes destroyed the citrus industry in the region, and began promoting the area as a winter resort for his friends in the North. Quickly constructing several small hotels, he hired the Scottish golf professional John Duncan Dunn to design a nine-hole golf course for his friends to play. By the spring of 1914, Morse's efforts had become so successful that he closed that course, and he and several friends incorporated the Winter Park Country Club. A new course was laid out and a clubhouse built. Incorporation allowed them to restrict membership and to limit membership to only those persons who were part of their social circle.

In 1907, citrus pioneer William J. Howey, fresh from Mexico, started new agricultural programs in Polk County, near Winter Haven and Lake Hamilton. In 1914, however, he shifted his operations to Lake County, north of Orlando, and began buying up acreage for the purpose of creating small citrus farms to sell to new residents. By 1917, he owned more than sixty thousand acres and was poised to undertake marketing in a big way.

Left: Circus entrepreneur John Ringling came to Sarasota in 1911, and by 1917, he owned more than sixty thousand acres of raw land. *Courtesy of the Florida Historical Society*.

Below: By the early 1920s, John and Mabel Ringling were social and financial leaders in the small town of Sarasota. They built an opulent mansion, Cà d'Zan, which mirrored the style of James Deering's Vizcaya in Miami. Although John's brother Charles also built a mansion, it could not compare with Cà d'Zan. *Courtesy of the Florida Historical Society*.

World War I intervened, however, and Howey's plans had to be scaled back. In 1914, Frederick Ruth, a native of Maryland and an executive with the Alabama Power and Light Company, left the world of business and came to Lake Wales to see what economic opportunities might be found in managing the thirteen hundred acres of open land his late father had purchased in 1883. With two friends, James Mitchell and James Washburn, he created the planned community of Mountain Lake. Once again, the outbreak of the Great War slowed plans for development, although the noted landscape designer Frederick Law Olmsted Jr. created a master plan for closely regulated growth. The restrictions brought about by the outbreak of war certainly meant disappointment for these developers, but the pump was primed for rapid expansion in the future.

In other parts of Florida, other wealthy investors claimed their share of the Sunshine State. In 1919, three Cleveland, Ohio residents—Dr. J.P. Sawyer, Edgar Strong and Dr. W.H. Humiston—purchased 160 acres of land on the barrier island directly across the Indian River Lagoon from the small mainland community of Vero. Separated by the Indian River from the mainland, the property, first known as Southern Dunes, would become one of the most exclusive enclaves in the Sunshine State, restricted to families that met the social and financial standards of the original founders. The founders quickly began to build large homes—most without kitchens—in the development. Residents took their meals at the clubhouse, which was completed in 1919. A few years later Arthur McKee, a prominent local promoter, was the first guest to stay in the clubhouse and built the first home in the development in 1919. Six additional homes were soon finished. Among the first homes constructed that year was "Orchid Oaks," built by New York attorney Winchester Fitch, who suggested that the community's name be changed from Southern Dunes to the Riomar Country Club, a combination of the Spanish words for river and sea.

On the west coast, Ransom E. Olds, a major automobile manufacturer, purchased 37,541 acres of land in Pinellas County in 1913. Olds set out to establish a farming community for workers who retired from his factories. Although Olds sold his development to Harold Prettyman in 1923, his vision of a town based on small-scale model farms continued to prosper until the latter years of that decade.

Despite the rapid growth of small and exclusive developments in the Sunshine State, there was little cohesiveness in the overall designs or marketing efforts of the new communities. Developers saw the Florida landscape as a blank canvas, and each brought his own tastes to the projects.

Originally intended to serve as a hospital for wounded American soldiers but never used as such, this Addison Mizner–designed building was converted into the Everglades Club by Paris Singer, the wealthy philanthropist who commissioned it. Admission to the Everglades Club was highly prized, and membership served to confirm one's social standing in Palm Beach. *Courtesy of the Florida Historical Society.*

From English Tudor and Italian Rococo to Cape Cod cottage and rustic Quaker farmhouse, prospective buyers were presented a veritable feast of styles from which to choose. This individualistic approach to development design was a hallmark of Florida development in the first two decades of the twentieth century, but this was about to change.

In well-established Palm Beach, the mercurial Addison Mizner, an untrained but talented architect, accepted a commission from his friend, Paris Singer, to design and build a hospital for wounded soldiers. Drawing on his experiences in Latin America and Europe, Mizner constructed a large building with a combination of old Spanish missions and Mediterranean towers. The war ended before the hospital was completed, and Singer decided to open the building as the Everglades Club, a facility that would be restricted to only those members he considered worthy. As a result, Singer became the arbiter of Palm Beach society, filling the same role Ward McAllister had performed in the 1890s in New York.

Mizner's design for the Everglades Club took Palm Beach by storm, and when he created a thirty-seven-room "cottage" for Mrs. Edward T. Stotesbury, the acknowledged queen of the local society, he ignited a major revolution in Palm Beach and dramatically altered the immediate future of architectural design in the Sunshine State. For Palm Beach, the "hotel civilization" was replaced by a more permanent culture of elaborate, "damn the cost" winter homes that rivaled those of Newport in size and expense. Instead of more traditional American forms of architecture or the copies of European palaces that dominated there, Palm Beach houses featured the distinctive quasi-Mediterranean styles introduced by Mizner. For the rest of Florida, the majority of homes—large and small—built during the next twenty years would be derivatives of this "bastard" form of architecture, persisting in most upscale subdivisions until today. Mizner's "new-old" architectural style appeared at just the right time, and his style became the face of Florida in the popular mind during the boom of the 1920s.

CHAPTER 3

World War Primes the Pump Even More

The boom began at the psychological moment when its repercussion on the rest of America was most likely to be felt. It began at a time when there was more money in the United States than there had ever been before, at a time when the infinitely smaller boom in California had already lost a great part of its novelty, and at a time when the almost universal adoption of the automobile made possible a nation-wide trek unthinkable in the days of the Alaskan gold-rushes and the booms in the Middle-West. The Florida boom, too, had the inestimable advantage of being advertised on a scale, and with a degree of skill, which had never previously been approached in the advertising of any similar activity. And Florida, though having been to a large extent actually created out of worthless swamps and impassable bogs by the skill and capital of its engineers, had about it the additional glamour of an absolutely untested intrinsic value. Nobody knew what Florida land was actually worth, apart from boom conditions; nobody knows even to this day.

—*T.H. Weigall,* Boom in Paradise, *1932*

By the end of the 1890s, a growing class of professional business managers oversaw the giant corporations of the robber barons, and while they did not accrue the vast fortunes of the super rich, they did have significant amounts of disposable income that afforded them the opportunity to take vacations and to participate in the "good life." Thorstein Veblen, looking at the emergence of the middle class during this period, labeled it the "leisure class," obsessed with conspicuous consumption—a designation that was very apt. "The quasi-peaceable gentleman of leisure, then, not only consumes of the staff of life beyond the minimum required for subsistence and physical efficiency," he wrote in *The Theory of the Leisure Class* (1899),

> *but his consumption also undergoes a specialization as regards the quality of the goods consumed. He consumes freely and of the best, in food, drink, narcotics, shelter, services, ornaments, apparel, weapons and accoutrements, amusements, amulets, and idols or divinities. In the process of gradual amelioration which takes place in the articles of his consumption, the motive principle and proximate aim of innovation is no doubt the higher efficiency of the improved and more elaborate products for personal comfort and well-being. But that does not remain the sole purpose of their consumption. The canon of reputability is at hand and seizes upon such innovations as are, according to its standard, fit to survive.* Since the consumption of these more excellent goods is an evidence of wealth, it becomes honorific; and conversely, the failure to consume in due quantity and quality becomes a mark of inferiority and demerit [emphasis added].

Several important factors explain the emergence of the large middle class in the United States, and without all of them being present in a short time frame, American society would not have changed much. Each of these factors contributed to the explosion in land sales that made up the Florida boom of the early 1920s.

First, American industry, unlike its European counterpart, quickly accepted the idea of mass production, sacrificing the idea of skilled workmen starting and finishing the same project for the process whereby many different people worked on an assembly line, creating a finished product made out of interchangeable parts. Mass production was the brainchild of American inventor Eli Whitney, who applied the technique to manufacture guns in antebellum America. Although the technique was slow to catch on, the urgent demand for millions of units of the same items created by the Civil War ensured its triumph in industry. In the post–Civil War period, techniques for mass production were refined as a growing population demanded more goods and services. It was Henry Ford, however, who popularized the method in his factories in Detroit. He was so successful that Ford cars dominated the American market.

Ford was also responsible for boosting the status of laborers in the United States when he offered to pay his factory workers five dollars a day. This was unheard of when he inaugurated his pay scale, but he argued that his workers were also his customers and that he wanted to pay them enough to be able to buy a Ford car, which cost about $250 before World War I. Once Ford had implemented his revolutionary wage program, other manufacturers in all industries felt forced to go along. American workers were the highest-paid workers in the world.

Second, the "trust busting" efforts of President Theodore Roosevelt and the Progressive Party during the first decade of the 1900s had broken up into smaller companies the large monopolies that dominated American business. With the breakup, the level of competition grew as smaller companies entered the marketplace. As a corollary to business expansion, the number of midlevel managers and business professionals grew, and the American middle class expanded. In a few colleges in the United States, small business schools emerged to teach the "scientific" principles of management.

Third, during the first two decades of the twentieth century, the installment plan became the favorite American way to purchase goods, including automobiles. Although a variation of this had been in place for several decades, the earlier version required purchasers to make small payments until the item was fully paid for before taking possession of it. The new version allowed the consumer to get the item and use it while payments were made. As long as the installment payments were made on time, the consumer could claim ownership. If payments were missed, however, the original seller/lender repossessed and resold the item. By using a variation of the "dollar-a-week" plan, American society became a consumer society—once again taking a different path than European societies. For the first time in American history, everyone—from the poorest farmer to the wealthiest Wall Street magnate—had a stake in the wave of prosperity that swept over the United States in the early 1920s. The increasing popularity of the automobile made it possible for virtually every class in society to pick up and move. Funded through "installment" plans created by banks and manufacturers, just about every American could acquire items that had previously been available only to the wealthiest—cars, appliances and consumer goods of all sorts. Henry Ford took advantage of this new method of financing, and by producing the reliable and inexpensive "flivver," he is credited with creating the "car culture" in the United States.

The installment plan became so prominent in American business that few areas of economic activity escaped. During the boom of the 1920s, most speculative purchases of Florida land were bought with a "little down and small weekly or monthly payments." With a small down payment, usually 5 or 10 percent of the total selling price, purchasers gained control of the property in question and, although state law forbade the resale of the property until the title change had been duly recorded, would quickly resell it for an increased price. Frequently, a property would change hands several times in the course of a day or a week. For purchasers of homes, the installment plan worked as well. A small down payment and monthly payments for twenty or so years were enough to secure a permanent or seasonal domicile in paradise.

Another important factor in paving the way for the real estate bonanza that dominated the Sunshine State in the 1920s was the tremendous wave of prosperity for American industry that accompanied World War I. The United States entered the war in 1917, three years after the first fighting broke out in Europe. The sale of war materiel to the countries united against Germany injected tremendous amounts of money into the U.S. economy, which grew exponentially when America finally entered the war. Labor shortages due to the draft of more than one million American youths created increasing demands for more labor, which produced a corresponding increase in wages paid to workers.

When the war ended on November 11, 1918, the war-weary Europeans faced the tasks of restructuring destroyed industries and paying off the enormous debts accrued to finance the war effort. Germany, judged the sole country responsible for starting the war by the victorious powers, faced heavy reparations. Its industry, which had rivaled that of the United States prior to the outbreak, faced severe restrictions on the items that it was allowed to produce, accelerated inflation that made German currency worthless and a severe shortage of manpower because of the 1.5 million deaths (roughly 15.3 percent of its male population) it suffered. France, Russia, Belgium, Great Britain and other countries suffered similar losses and faced many of the same problems.

The United States' casualties for the eighteen-month period of its involvement numbered 115,000. While relatively small when compared to European countries, the number of men permanently removed from the workforce created problems for manufacturers. The large number of men who came back from the war and sought time to decompress from the rigors of warfare further exacerbated the situation. War-weary veterans, tired of calls for duty and addicted to the adrenalin rush of battle, looked for new forms of excitement in their lives that could replace the dangers of warfare.

World War I also proved the superiority of machines over animal power. Many a doughboy who had grown up in rural America gained his

In the immediate postwar period, thousands of tin canners took to American roads, with many using surplus military tents and vehicles. Florida, particularly the large and wild areas in the center of the state, was a popular destination. *Courtesy of the Florida Historical Society.*

first exposure to the widespread use of machines powered by the internal combustion engine—tanks, automobiles and airplanes. With the end of the war, large quantities of surplus government equipment flooded the American marketplace at prices that made it possible for the public to acquire these items at prices well below the cost of new ones. As a result, Americans hit the road using surplus government automobiles, equipped with surplus tents, camp stoves and tools, seeking to explore the last frontiers of North America. They joined a growing group of automobile tourists, commonly referred to as the "tin canners."

Although railroads and steamboats in the late 1800s opened the east and west coasts of the peninsula to visitors, the center of the state experienced little in the way of tourism or large-scale settlement. No single area was as representative of frontier America as the Sunshine State. For decades, Florida slept tranquilly under the hot tropical sun, occasionally aroused by seasonal influxes of tourists but generally left to its own devices. Large areas of uninhabited land in the interior of the peninsula provided a frontier atmosphere where scraggly cattle, herded by dangerous-looking cowhands, were the most likely sights a visitor would see. For every Ormond Beach, Tampa, Palm Beach or Miami that offered a destination for the wealthy, there were hundreds of small towns, surrounded by tropical hammocks and open plains, that were important only to their residents.

The automobile freed visitors from the straight lines of railroads and the often unfavorable locations of rivers, and as a result of these freewheeling explorers, vast sections of the Florida interior were opened to tourism. Life as a tin canner meant few hotels, fewer service centers and even fewer tourist attractions. Not bound by roads or reason, these original "off-roaders" carved new destinations for tourists in Florida. Because few amenities were in place, early auto tourists carried extra gasoline, tires, repair kits, tents and food with them. "They came to Florida with $10 and an extra pair of underwear, and when they left six weeks later they had changed neither," went a popular joke of the period. They all shared this common experience, and in 1919, a group met in de Soto Park in Tampa to form the Tin Can Tourists of the World, a social group that still exists today.

The automobile also offered Americans a new sense of privacy. No longer bound by the fixed routes of railroads—where newspapers in towns along the routes frequently published the names and business of new arrivals—automobile tourists came and went as they pleased without having to meet the schedules of other people. The passage of the Eighteenth Amendment and the Volstead Act in 1919 ushered in the Prohibition era in the United States, which many Americans interpreted as a direct assault on their individual rights and an invasion of their privacy. Florida's proximity to Bimini, Cuba and Bermuda guaranteed the supply of illicit liquor for rumrunners, while the tacit consent of revenue agents allowed its availability to clubs and restaurants in the state—reinforcing the growing perception of the state as a play land. While Europe was still rebuilding from the destruction of World War I, the United States entered into a fast-paced, hedonistic era known as the Jazz Age. Fueled by new and available technology—radio, telephones, airplanes, movies and electricity—and serenaded by the formerly forbidden music of Negro brothels in New Orleans and St. Louis, America was on the move, ready to see new places and do new things. The craving for unusual experiences sparked a new society that rejected the old and staid values of the nineteenth century and advocated "change for change's sake."

The success of the Good Roads Movement, originally started in the 1880s as a movement to create new and better roads for bicyclists, gained

The ratification of the Eighteenth Amendment and the passage of the Volstead Act ushered in the Prohibition era in the United States. Americans quickly turned to bootlegging and rumrunning. Florida's proximity to Bimini, Cuba and Bermuda made it an ideal base for rumrunners. *Courtesy of the Tampa-Hillsborough County Public Library.*

momentum in the years immediately before the war. In 1913, Carl Fisher, who would become the Sunshine State's wealthiest land promoter in the 1920s, sought to create a coast-to-coast highway across the United States. Although not an immediate success, the proposed Lincoln Highway generated a great deal of favorable publicity and the support of hundreds of cities and towns that hoped for the economic stimulus such a road would bring. In 1915, Fisher and other Good Road advocates created the Montreal-to-Miami highway, which opened to great fanfare. While crude in its construction, the road nevertheless made it possible to drive from Canada to Miami in a few days. For several years, the Dixie Highway, as it was popularly known, was the major automobile route into Florida. During the Great War, the federal government quickly realized the need for a complex system of good highways in order to accommodate the movement of men and equipment for military purposes. Within a few years, the United States was crisscrossed by a network of passable roads.

Floridians quickly noted the influx of tin canners into the state as another potential source of tourist revenues and just as quickly developed roadside

The popularity of bicycling in the United States and the need for better transportation routes for industry and travel led to the Good Roads Movement. *Courtesy of the Tampa-Hillsborough County Library System.*

attractions to lure them to particular destinations. Alligators, ostriches, giant trees and natural springs, as well as the natural flora and fauna of the Sunshine State, became the focus of roadside advertisements. Mom and pop fruit stands and general stores, some selling gasoline or offering tire repairs or the services of mechanics, provided pleasant stops along the roads. St. Augustine, drawing on its Spanish heritage, became a tourist mecca, where the nation's oldest surviving house attracted as much attention as Ponce de León's mythical Fountain of Youth (which moved several times). Seminole villages, deep in the Everglades, were largely inaccessible, so the Indians moved them closer to the roads.

Tourist homes—small inns dedicated to the touring public—operated in most small towns and cities. Small hotels also expanded their offerings, and for the first time, the pleasures and destinations of America's rich were available—in a slightly limited fashion—to scads of middle-class citizens. Sports like golf, tennis and croquet, long considered the domain of the very wealthy, were democratized as hoteliers began marketing their hotels

Above: As the automobile tourists flooded into Florida, enterprising residents developed a variety of small attractions to get them to stop and spend money. This is an alligator farm in north Florida, near St. Augustine. *Florida State Photographic Archives*.

Below: Mom and pop fruit stands and general stores provided weary automobile travelers with pleasant places to stop, rest and, of course, spend money. *Courtesy of the Florida Historical Society*.

The small villages of Florida's Seminole Indians, located in the Everglades, were favorite places to visit for tourists in the 1920s. For the Seminoles, tourists provided an extra source of income. *Courtesy of the Moorhead Collection.*

specifically to the middle class. Although the number of extremely rich Americans grew rapidly during the second half of the nineteenth century, their numbers were small when compared to those of the middle class. If Florida promoters could attract this newly affluent group of Americans to the Sunshine State, they could use the sheer numbers of the middle class, who spent less money overall, to more than make up for the extravagant expenditures of the fewer numbers of the fabulously wealthy.

Finally, the large numbers of service personnel who trained in military bases around the state during the war carried the message of how exciting life in the Sunshine State could be to thousands of friends and relatives back home when the war was over. Their enthusiasm for Florida was no different from that of servicemen who had come south in other wars and who would train in Florida in future wars. They carried the message of perpetual sunshine, open spaces and year-round warm weather—which had been and would continue to be the message of advertisements for the state—to northern residents, tired of cold winters, increasing populations and urban sprawl. Once again, the pump was being primed.

CHAPTER 4

The Truth about Florida Is a Lie!

At a meeting of Florida advertising men, trying to formulate a program for presenting the facts about the state to the outside world, a few years ago, suggestion after suggestion was rejected because it was felt that the contemplated statement, though true, would not be accepted as truth. Finally one of the group summed up the matter in a phrase that has become historic: "Gentlemen," he said, "the truth about Florida is a lie!"

—*Frank Parker Stockbridge and John Holliday Perry,*
Florida in the Making, *1926*

The Florida land boom of the 1920s funneled thousands of additional people into the Sunshine State. This time, however, they came with a different purpose—not to settle permanently but to capitalize on the real estate boom. A second wave of industrialists, flush with the profits of wartime manufacturing, looked for new places to build second and third homes. The first generation of middle-class managers, similarly flush with extra money, sought to emulate their "betters" and cast about for new ways and new places to flaunt their newly gotten wealth. While Europe had served as a prewar haven for the wealthy and the wannabes, the war, with its violence and destruction, made the continent less than desirable. Florida, with its endless beaches, perpetual sunshine and exotic locales, beckoned. The open spaces and cheap land made it an attractive clean slate where the nouveau riche and established moneyed families could bring their wildest dreams into reality. For those who simply wanted to belong and whose imagination was limited, hundreds of architects and thousands of builders were willing to design and build houses that rivaled the best Europe had to offer.

When the end of World War I sent the American economy on an upward surge that would last throughout the decade of the 1920s, Florida was among the first beneficiaries of the new prosperity. Immediately after the end of hostilities, Americans began to flock to the Sunshine State, enticed by the advertising departments of the great railroads that skimmed both coasts and by the excitement through firsthand experiences by the automobile tourists who plunged headlong into the vast and largely unexplored wilderness of the central peninsula.

The economic descendants of Henry Flagler and Henry Plant, now concerned with recovering the tremendous expenses of running railroads the length of the state, saw the exploitation of large tracts of land as the best chance of bolstering the fortunes of the Florida East Coast Railroad and the Plant System. The railroads controlled large blocks of land, awarded as compensation for railroad construction by the state and federal governments and the key to continued prosperity for these entities. Other companies and individuals eagerly sought to ride on the shoulders of the railroads and purchased huge acreages, ready to take a chance on whatever the future brought—and what the '20s brought to Florida was people and more people!

For hundreds of thousands of Americans, Florida captured the spirit of the Jazz Age. It was virgin territory that could be shaped to fit the desires of a restless population. Unfettered by the strictures of older societies in the East and Midwest, and somewhat insulated from the conservatism of the agricultural South, Florida was a tabula rasa that could and would be whatever the new owners wanted it to be.

The boom in Florida lands meant that a mighty torrent of people was pushing south, seeking the latest American El Dorado. As trains crossed the Georgia line, they were met by hordes of "binder boys," real estate agents who carried hundreds of deeds with them—all for sale to a willing public. Between Jacksonville and Miami, some 350 miles, a single deed might be bought and sold several times and then sold several more times between the last train station and the nearest hotel. Unseen, unsurveyed and unsettled, land was important only as a commodity that could be bought and sold rapidly for a profit. "The only person who doesn't make money on Florida land," remarked one wag, "is the man who doesn't own any."

Binder boys of all ages boarded southbound trains in Jacksonville with full briefcases of deeds. As the trains rolled south across the Georgia-Florida

Left: By 1924, promoters in Florida advertised in most of the nation's newspapers and magazines. For those who were too busy or too far away to come to the Sunshine State immediately, purchasing a homestead by mail was a quick and easy thing to do. *Courtesy of Special Collections, University of South Florida.*

Below: Florida's flat topography and lack of hard, rocky soil allowed developers to shape and mold it into whatever configuration they desired. Here workers clear palmettos and other brush from the site of the future town of Oldsmar. *Courtesy of the Tampa-Hillsborough County Library System.*

border, there was an active trade in deeds, and it was not unusual for a single deed to be bought and sold ten or fifteen times as the train rolled south or another ten or more times before the last purchaser had arrived at his hotel after exiting the train. Al Trafford, an old-time resident of Cocoa and the owner of a realty company, recalls, "My father would meet the train each morning and board with a satchel full of deeds. He would return that evening with an empty bag. The next morning he would meet the train again and repeat the process. This went on for four or five years."

T.H. Weigall described how the system worked in his recollections of Miami during the apex of the land boom:

> *Towards the end of the year* [1925], *the rush for land at any price reached such insane proportions that the "binder Boys" used to meet the trains bringing fresh arrivals from the north, and often enough sell the alleged options for cash even before their clients had left the railway station. I am not suggesting that the majority of these options were not perfectly genuine, as indeed most of them were; but the complications attaching to them were in nearly every case so hopelessly involved that in the event of anyone actually wanting to take possession of the property (a very remote contingency) the difficulties would have been almost unthinkable.*

For serious developers like Carl Fisher and George Merrick, the activities of the binder boys brought chaos to the marketplace, but the energy and excitement they generated translated into more interest in large-scale communities like Miami Beach and Coral Gables. The unlicensed binder boys also created havoc for professional real estate agents denied a commission of the informal sales and for government officials charged with recording land transactions. Although Florida law specified that a resale could not take place until the first sale was duly recorded in the county clerk's office, the reality was that, during the early years of the boom, a single deed might change hands five or six times in a single day. Newspapers were full of stories about the tremendous fortunes made by speculators, and no claim was so absurd as to be ignored. One story that appeared several times in various papers featured a young bank clerk who arrived in Miami on a ten o'clock train, purchased a property from one of the notorious binder boys, sold it to another person without leaving the train station and caught the next train north with a profit of $15,000 in his pocket. True? Perhaps. Try as they might to eliminate them, binder boys remained a fact of life throughout the boom. By 1926, however, professional real estate agents (and the staffs of developers) had gained the upper hand, and the number of binder boys decreased.

The costs of developing raw land into subdivisions were enormous, and an explosion of bankers, banks and banking accompanied the land frenzy. Historically, banking in the Sunshine State was problematic. Given the legacy of the nineteenth-century frontier and Andrew Jackson's epic struggle with Nicholas Biddle's Bank of the United States, banks and bankers were usually regarded with a great deal of suspicion. The failure of the Union Bank in 1843 and the subsequent indebtedness brought about by the Civil War reinforced the general anti-bank sentiments of Floridians. Despite the innate distrust of banks in the Sunshine State, they were necessary elements in fueling and funding the boom of the 1920s. In 1920, Florida's banking community had deposits in federal banks that totaled a mere $61 million, only slightly more than Mississippi's $53.3 million. However, the Standard Statistic Company of New York reported that the consolidated total for both national and federal banks that year was $187 million. By 1924, the amount of deposits in Florida banks had grown to $263 million. By 1925, Miami banks alone counted more than $60 million in deposits, while Tampa banks reported an additional $25 million. In Palm Beach, bank deposits exceeded $5 million, while total bank deposits in Jacksonville in May 1925 also passed the $5 million mark. The aggregate total of deposits for that year exceeded $375 million.

After 1920, scores of new state and federal banks opened to receive deposits of monies paid on land purchases and to lend money for development. Between 1920 and 1929, some 127 new state banks were chartered and 36 new national banks received charters. Raymond Vickers, in his seminal book *Panic in Paradise: Florida's Banking Crash of 1926*, documents the "iffy" nature of Florida banks, which were poorly funded and suffered from dubious dealings from organizers. Vickers also documents the unsound practices of interlocking directorates, the transfer of funds from "corresponding" banks, the looting of bank resources by bank officers and the criminal—although unprosecuted—actions by state regulators who took advantage of their positions to gain unsecured loans. These transgressions would become apparent after the real estate bubble burst in 1926, but until that time, Florida's bankers assured depositors and investors alike that there was no end to prosperity, all the while using their state and federal banks as personal cash registers.

Although some developers, like Carl Fisher and Glenn H. Curtiss, were millionaires before the Florida boom began in 1920 and brought their money with them, the majority of the big players depended on loans from banks. In 1925, banks committed $300 million—or roughly 80 percent of all deposits—for real estate development in the Sunshine State. As developers sought to implement more and more grandiose plans, they raised the percentage of the purchase price for land and houses by as much as 20 percent. The cash generated was put back into development, while promissory notes for the remainder provided the collateral for bank loans to pay for additional expansion.

Much of the money placed in Florida banks came from outside the state. In order to encourage investment from inside and outside the state, banks and chambers of commerce around the state prevailed upon the legislature to place an amendment on the ballot to prohibit the collection of a state income tax, which was approved in the November 1924 general election. In the same election, Florida residents voted to abolish the state inheritance tax in the mistaken belief that this would encourage more investments in the state. However, since the Revenue Act of 1924 allowed for up to 80 percent of any inheritance taxes paid to a state to be deducted from the federal taxes due, the repeal of the state law governing inheritance taxes deprived Florida of badly needed income. In their eagerness to cater to investors, Florida legislators had shot themselves in the foot. The Florida amendment was subsequently repealed in 1930.

Traditional individual borrowers who wanted to finance their home purchases did so at an annual average interest rate of 8 percent for ten or fifteen years, with a 25 percent down payment and a 5 percent bonus to the bank making the loan. According to a report issued by the Standard Statistic Company, "Unless there is to be continued a rather rapid enhancement in real estate values, this interest rate is likely to work very considerable hardship on a purchaser." Of course, the company continued, "If the buyer is able to place his property immediately on the market and sell, this is not a matter of serious concern, but otherwise he stands a fair chance of having to hold on to a non-income property, the carrying charge on which is high."

Still, the report continued, there were 35 million acres of land in the Sunshine State, and 22 million were "capable of development." Nevertheless, the report concluded that "local trades and industries" required to service a rapidly growing population offered the best investment opportunities for the post-1925 era. While acknowledging that some of the early developers would continue to reap profits, the report warned that "the boom has reached the stage where the greatest future profits will be realized not so much from ventures in real estate, as from carefully considered investments in sound business or industrial concerns."

In 1926, Frank Parker Stockbridge, a journalist, with the cooperation of John Holliday Perry, a Florida banker and journalist, coauthored *Florida in the Making*, a book with the specific purpose of convincing Americans of the underlying solidity and safety of investing in Florida real estate. Published prior to the devastating hurricane of that year and the subsequent bank failures that accompanied it, the authors assured readers that "the very existence of speculative activity implies the existence of underlying values. One might well ask whether the Stock Exchange rests upon a sound and stable base. Speculation in stocks would cease were there no values behind the share traded in." Governor John W. Martin, a Jacksonville lawyer with strong banking ties, praised the authors for their efforts. "The sun of Florida's destiny has arisen," he wrote in the foreword, "and only the malicious and the short-sighted contend or believe that it will ever set. Marvellous [*sic*] as is the wonder-story of Florida's recent achievements, these are but heralds of the dawn." Martin promised "that all which has yet been done in Florida is but a beginning toward what is to come." Prophetic words, indeed.

CHAPTER 5

Going Full Bore
SELLING THE BOOM

Then the land rush began. Thousands upon thousands of people, attracted by the stories of wealth made over-night, began the hopeful trek to Florida. In cities and towns men sold out their small shops; on western prairies and New England hillsides families disposed of their holdings; waiters, clerks, salesmen, writers, lawyers, mechanics and medicine men, all fevered by a dream of wealth, formed an astounding cavalcade of teams and trains and motor cars, dribbling from all parts of the Union into the glutted highways of Florida. Sanity fled the scene; Tom o' Bedlam was the uncrowned king; caution and common sense were out of hand and out of mind. Folly was rife.
—Burton Rascoe, Introduction, Boom in Paradise, *1932*

With a system of banks in place and a statewide atmosphere of favorable financing for even the most extreme project, Florida's land boom exploded and reached its zenith in 1924 and 1925. More than one million people flocked to the Sunshine State each year to sample the excitement of America's tame frontier. Florida was where the action was, where all the "best" people came and where the "in crowd" of movie stars, politicians, literary icons and athletes could be found whiling away the days playing golf, betting on the horses, dancing all night at exotic nightclubs or engaging in some other "go-go" activity. Not even the golden sunshine of California or the French Riviera could compare to that of Florida, and Californians and Europeans abandoned their slices of paradise to come to the Sunshine State. Once they had crossed the state's borders, many of these arrivals were caught up in the hurly-burly that was the boom. It was too difficult to escape the economic tumult that saw instant millionaires created overnight or to forego the opportunity to rub elbows with the famous and powerful. The possibility of becoming a part of the new American elite attracted both the possessors of old money and the renters of new money. Speculation on the stock market, involvement in criminal activities like Prohibition and the installment plan made it difficult to distinguish the newly rich wannabes from the established upper crust. The Florida boom was, in the words of one observer, "truly a democratizing experience."

To keep the image of Florida as a hub of activity, large-scale developers like Carl Fisher and George Merrick employed a large staff of in-house publicists who worked around the clock to ballyhoo the achievements of their employers. Newspapers and magazines of the era, eager to save money without having to employ reporters and facing empty pages, faithfully reprinted the press releases they received from them. T.H. Weigall, a British expatriate who worked for the Merrick organization in 1925, described the advertising department to which he was assigned: "The main feature of the Advertising Department was a vast battery of electric duplicating machines,

By trains, boats, cars and even airplanes, Americans flocked to the Sunshine State in the early 1920s. Florida promised a freewheeling atmosphere when rich and poor, famous and infamous, nouveau riche and scions of European thrones mixed freely and engaged in land speculation. *Florida State Photographic Archives.*

with double crews working three eight-hour shifts all through the twenty-four hours." Out of this "Niagara" of propaganda came letters written by machines, press releases, posters and circulars of all kinds.

> *The crudity and blatancy of many of the poster designs were past belief. The majority of these depicted an entirely mythical city, with gleaming spires and glistening domes making up an idealized blend of Moscow and Oxford, with the exception that they were invariably rising out of a tropical paradise in which lovely ladies and marvelously-dressed gallants disported themselves under the palm-trees.*

Representing a concoction of free-reign imaginations and outright lying,

> *such pictures scarcely ever bore the slightest relation to the dreary flats, occasionally intersected by a few hundred yards of white way lighting…It is scarcely possible to believe that the gullibility of the American public was so unlimited that these incredible pictures could ever have been taken for even a remote resemblance to reality.*

Yet believe them the American public did.

Every Florida promoter, large and small, used buses, limousines and trams to transport prospective buyers from their hotels to the sites of new developments. This is Wallace Stovall's Tampa Beach development, circa 1925. Buses brought potential buyers to the site several times a day. *Courtesy of the Tampa-Hillsborough County Library System.*

Developers also created trolley lines to bring local visitors and residents to their subdivisions. Larger developers, like Merrick, Fisher, Mizner, Curtiss and Davis, also created their own bus lines, which regularly fetched potential buyers from Montgomery, Atlanta and a dozen other southern cities. On special occasions, these lines were extended as far away as New York City, Chicago and San Francisco. Expensive to operate, such bus lines were considered to be good investments because of the substantial increases in home purchases they engendered.

Between 1920 and 1930, Florida moved from being the thirty-second ranked state in population to the thirty-first. More people became permanent residents in the Sunshine State between 1920 and 1925 than during the previous ten years. So many people wanted to come to Florida during this five-year period that railroads embargoed cargoes of nonperishable goods, and the highways were crowded with tourists and persons seeking to invest in development.

Tampa's population rose by 84 percent; the number of permanent residents in Miami increased an amazing 165 percent; Lakeland, Orlando and West Palm Beach saw increases of 142, 140 and 121 percent, respectively, during the same five-year period. Cities like Jacksonville, Tallahassee and Pensacola, located in the northern section of the state, experienced the lowest growth rates of all—between 3 and 20 percent. Overall, however, the growth rate for the United States was only 7 percent between 1920 and 1925, while Florida's rate of growth was 29 percent, or four times the national average.

CITY GROWTH IN FLORIDA, 1920–1925

CITY	1920	1925	% INCREASE
Tampa	51,608	94,808	84%
Jacksonville	91,558	94,206	3%
Miami	29,571	71,419	165%
Lakeland	7,062	17,064	142%
Orlando	9,282	22,272	140%
West Palm Beach	8,659	19,132	121%

Florida was different, and its rapidly growing population demanded a new identity that reflected its uniqueness. Part of this new identity could be found in the advertisements of the era, which incorporated the sun, the beach, the automobile, the golf course and the idea of a perpetual vacation into a single poster or magazine cover.

For most newcomers, however, the excitement generated by the promoters and developers could not be assuaged with the construction of homes like those left in the northern states or by traditional American architecture. Instead, they looked to the older civilizations of the Mediterranean—the Romans, Greeks, Spanish and North Africans—for inspiration. What could be more exotic or desirable than a fabled recreation of the sunny playgrounds of wealthy Europeans? In Boca Raton, Addison Mizner, lately of the Alaskan gold fields, became the "god" of Florida architecture as he vigorously promoted his ideas of "Mediterranean revival" as a perfect fit for the endless sunny days of Florida. Mizner's ability to paint a picture of "new" Florida perfectly blended into Old Europe answered the need for something truly different from the ordinary. According to David Nolan, Mizner explained his architectural vision thusly: "I sometimes start a house with a Romanesque corner, pretend that it has fallen into disrepair and been added to in the Gothic spirit, when suddenly the great wealth of the New World has poured in and the owner had added a very rich Renaissance addition." Above all, he concluded, it was necessary to remember that "these people can't stand the sight of anything that doesn't cost a lot of money."

He persuaded his wealthy clients to purchase antiques, paintings and furnishings of all kinds from Tuscany, Venice, Sicily or Greece. Soon, entire rooms of Mediterranean furniture, architectural elements and art found their way to Boca Raton for incorporation into a Mizner-built home. What he could not purchase abroad, he manufactured in his own studios—reproductions of ancient tiles, antique doors, murals and numerous other items that captured the feeling of Old Europe.

Another part of Florida's new identity came when most developers tacitly adopted an overarching style of architecture—Mediterranean Revival. Glenn Curtiss, the developer of Hialeah, preferred the adobe architecture of the American Southwest, but in the public's mind, there was little to distinguish it from the similar Mediterranean Revival. Some developers, like Carl Dann, thought other architectural styles were more appropriate to Florida's interior, and his Mount Plymouth Golf and Country Club development in Lake County featured "gingerbread houses" designed and built by Sam Stoltz, a former illustrator for a poultry magazine. Stoltz's homes were generally

The ornate Mediterranean Revival style of architecture, first popularized by Addison Mizner in Palm Beach, became the dominant architectural style of the Florida boom. This is the staircase at the Boca Club. *Courtesy of the Florida Historical Society.*

Tudor Revival in style but incorporated elements from Irish and Scottish country homes as well. Other, smaller developers also featured different architectural styles, but these proved less popular and ran counter to the public's perception of the Sunshine State.

Given Mizner's success in attracting the very wealthy as his clients in Boca Raton and Palm Beach, virtually every Florida developer immediately appropriated his ideas. On Florida's east and west coasts, where the majority of the money was being spent, Mediterranean Revival styles dominated. Davis Islands, the brainchild of "Doc" Davis in Tampa, who shamelessly promoted his development as a second Venice, was to replicate it completely with palazzos and canals. George Merrick even appropriated the name "Venetian Pool" for the community swimming pool in his Coral Gables development on the outskirts of Miami. Merrick, Davis, Fisher and Mizner aimed their developments at the very wealthy, but the majority of developers realized that the pool of the superrich was limited and sought to tailor their subdivisions or communities toward the moderately wealthy or upper middle class of American society. Whether they envisioned a restricted community of the superrich or a moderately priced development for the middle class, promoters of the Florida boom aimed at the vast dual markets of seasonal

Sam Stoltz, a Chicago architect, designed the "fantasy" houses for the Mount Plymouth Golf and Country Club development in Lake County. His designs were a deliberate attempt to make Mount Plymouth distinctive and stand out from the hundreds of Mediterranean Revival developments in the state. *Courtesy of the Florida Historical Society.*

visitors and permanent settlers, who equated the Sunshine State with the faux Mediterranean architecture.

Some promoters, like John and Charles Ringling in Sarasota, realized the need for new houses for the artisans, service personnel, laborers and merchants who provided the underpinnings of the more affluent society. These would be priced so that the workers could afford them, and a portion of their projects was reserved for these buyers. Even homes built for the working classes, however, followed the basic styles of Coral Gables, Miami Beach and Boca Raton. Many of the smaller homes featured inlaid tile floors, turrets or mini-towers and balconies. Other developments, like Oldsmar, founded by Ransom E. Olds for workers who retired from his factories, and Venice, owned in large part by the Brotherhood of Railroad Engineers, allowed families with modest incomes to buy into the Florida dream. Following the lead of promoters in Miami and Boca Raton, the developers of these communities adopted the Mediterranean Revival style of architecture so that the middle class could enjoy the feel of old Europe.

Hundreds of local developers throughout the state, awed by the money newcomers were willing to spend to buy a slice of these fantasies, quickly set their own architects to drawing plans for new "old" houses in distinctive

Not all developments in Florida during the boom featured expensive European-style homes. The "Quickbilt Bungalow" cost a mere $4,000 and could be erected in a single week. Such homes proved popular with members of the lower middle class. *Courtesy of Special Collections, University of South Florida.*

subdivisions. For those in a hurry to settle, some builders offered homes that could be erected in a week or ten days. Less substantial than the homes in the big South Florida developments, they nevertheless ensured that anyone, regardless of status, could have a piece of the Florida dream.

One of the most prolific, but underrated, architects of the 1920s was Richard Rummell, who resided in the small town of Rockledge and designed most of the public buildings and private homes in Brevard County during this decade. Unlike some of his peers, Rummell was formally educated as an architect in Pennsylvania and settled in Rockledge around 1915. Soon he became enamored with the new emphasis on Mediterranean Revival styles and worked with several local developers in the area to place Brevard County in the mainstream of the boom.

Rummell's work was largely concentrated on two developments. One was the Valencia Road development adjacent to the small downtown area of Rockledge and Virginia Park, which was located to the west of the neighboring city of Cocoa. Rummell also contributed designs for some houses in the small development of Carleton Terrace, which was part of the real estate empire of D.P. Davis and his brother, located about four miles north of Cocoa. In addition, Rummell designed the new governmental

Richard Rummell of Rockledge was an accomplished architect who adopted Mizner's Mediterranean Revival style in the early 1920s. He was a prolific worker and designed most of the boom-era houses in the Rockledge-Cocoa area, as well as the major public buildings. This is a typical home constructed during the boom using his architectural plans. *Courtesy of the Florida Historical Society*.

buildings for both cities. The demand for Mediterranean-style homes and public buildings kept him busy for several decades.

Craftsmen and carpenters, long used to building houses that featured wooden frame construction, suddenly found they had to solve new problems caused by terra cotta tile walls, heavy barrel-tiled roofs and ornately plastered walls, ceilings and decorative fireplaces. Wrought-iron stairs and balconies, foreign to earlier Florida homes, now became de rigueur and created a demand for entirely new construction skills. When local craftsmen could not master the new skills, workmen were brought in from northern states and, in the case of the homes of the wealthiest, from Europe. Soon, the broad Florida landscapes were filled with reproductions of European palaces, Spanish and Italian villas and even Moorish and Crusader castles.

The demands for building had an invigorating impact on the Florida economy, although it was limited somewhat to the middle and southern parts of the state. New industries, created to meet the demands of architects for elements for their designs, quickly emerged to supply building materials from Florida resources. The wave of apparent prosperity was not limited to buying and selling real estate but spilled over into other areas, particularly the service and hospitality sectors of the economy. Even old out-of-office politicians and sports figures, some long past their prime but still retaining some name recognition, found new employment as they became the handmaidens of promoters like Carl Fisher, George Merrick and D.P. "Doc" Davis, whose get-rich schemes moved from the banal to the blissful under the influence of these celebrities. Perhaps none of the promoters' promoters was more artful in selling than three-time presidential candidate and former secretary of state William Jennings Bryan, who, like some freak in a sideshow, dutifully pitched Merrick's Coral Gables development three times a day to large audiences. Merrick reportedly paid him $100,000 a year to front his development. Up and down the state, lesser-known figures made similar appeals pitching smaller developments—the only difference being one of scale not of content.

Golfing legends Walter Hagen and Bobby Jones lent their names and images to developments on the west coast—Jones in Sarasota and Hagen in St. Petersburg. John J. McGraw, persuaded by John Ringling to bring the New York Giants to Sarasota for spring training, soon joined the development craze and promoted his own subdivision, Pennant Park, where lots sold briskly. Jack Dempsey promoted Temple Terrace by staging exhibition-boxing matches, while President Warren G. Harding used his office and prestige to help promote Vero Beach and Miami Beach. Vice President Charles Dawes and his brother were major investors and promoters of Mizner's Boca Raton development, eventually taking over the Mizner operation entirely. President Calvin Coolidge also lent his prestige to various developments by simply visiting them, being photographed and then having his image reproduced in newspapers and magazines around the world. Countless other lesser lights added to the publicity mixture and created an energy-filled environment of "see and be seen."

The refusal of most Americans to abide by the Volstead Act and the glamour that often surrounded bootleggers made criminals like Captain William "Billy" McCoy, the premier smuggler of illegal alcohol from Bermuda, a welcomed guest at any hotel or resort. In virtually every major Florida city, booze was plentiful. Major developers like Carl Fisher, appalled at the federal government's regulation of personal freedom and aware that their livelihoods depended on keeping visitors happy, freely employed the services of bootleggers. As a matter of fact, Gar Wood, the famous racing boat driver for Fisher, lent his expertise about boats to rumrunners and, with Fisher's knowledge and approval, provided them with highly developed

Above: Famed orator and three-time presidential candidate William Jennings Bryan exhorted purchasers three times a day to buy property in George Merrick's Coral Gables. He received a $100,000 a year salary. He died in 1926. *Courtesy of the Florida Historical Society*.

Left: Bobby Jones, the all-time-best amateur golfer in history, frequently played courses in new developments in Florida during the 1920s. Although he never received payment or took cash prizes, he often demanded and received "gifts" from tournament sponsors. *Courtesy of the Moorhead Collection*.

One of the most famous athletes to play golf in Florida during the boom was George Herman "Babe" Ruth, an avid golfer. Ruth's presence in a tournament or an exhibition match was a surefire way to attract hordes of people to a development. *Courtesy of the Moorhead Collection*.

"Touts, louts and losers," so the local wisdom went, attended Hialeah daily to put their money on surefire winners. Glenn H. Curtiss, the developer of Hialeah, decided that the gambling environment was so strong it discouraged people from purchasing homes, and he subsequently built Country Club Estates and Opa-locka to appeal to families. *Courtesy of the Florida Historical Society*.

motors that would allow them to leave the Coast Guard in the distance on their almost nightly runs to the Bahamas, just sixty miles from Miami. In the words of Fisher's biographer, Mark Foster, "Carl did not simply tolerate rum-running into and out of Miami Beach; he became an active participant…He might have delegated the task of securing liquor to one of his managers, but Carl enjoyed running risks and matching wits with Prohibition agents."

Despite their reputations for violence, major crime figures were also accepted into the more gentrified society of boom-time Florida. The allure of associating with known criminals simply added additional zest to the already hectic 1920s. Mob boss Alphonse "Al" Capone, the king of Chicago crime, was a frequent visitor to Florida during the 1920s and reputedly lived on a boat in the Indian River, rented a large mansion in Mount Plymouth Golf and Country Club in Lake County for his gang, frequented the horse races in Hialeah and eventually purchased a mansion in Miami Beach. Carl Fisher later testified that Capone's presence as a Miami Beach resident contributed to the real estate collapse of the late '20s. Sam Cohen, who would later figure in the mob scandals in Las Vegas in the 1950s, came to Florida in the 1920s to establish bookmaking operations. Lesser figures in American crime came to Florida, particularly Miami and Tampa, to take advantage of the betting that surrounded such places as the infamous Beach Club in Palm Beach, the jai alai frontons in Miami and the thoroughbred horses at the Hialeah Race Course. Although illegal, gambling and gambling casinos operated in full view of the public and did so with the tacit approval of governmental authorities.

Everything—from the distinctive architecture to the colorful advertising brochures to the operations of illegal gambling establishments and rumrunners—contributed to creating a vision of Florida as the "Pleasure Paradise of the World," unmatched anywhere.

CHAPTER 6

A City from Whole Cloth

CARL GRAHAM FISHER

If ever a man made a city, Carl Fisher made Miami Beach—from the ground right up to its bathing beauties. Even today it still bears the stamp of his personality. So Miami begins with Carl Fisher.
—*Polly Redford,* Billion-Dollar Sandbar: A Biography of Miami Beach

It took a man with true vision to see America's playground emerging from the tidal swamps and sandy dunes on the small island on the northern shore of Biscayne Bay in 1913. It also took a man with great financial resources to translate his vision into reality. Yet, such a man was Carl Graham Fisher, an Indiana entrepreneur and marketing genius. From his fertile imagination—and with the help of round-the-clock dredges pumping millions of cubic yards of ocean sand onto the mangrove-lined shores—he created the paradise he had dreamed about. With broad streets edged with coconut palms, he platted individual lots for private homes, broad parks, bathhouses and polo-playing fields for visitors and residents in the new development of Alton Beach. By January 1914, it could boast of electrical and telephone services, and by December 1915, city water and sewage systems were in operation. To the north of his Alton Beach development, the Collins family and the Lummus brothers copied Fisher's efforts and added to the available pool of new acreage. In early 1915, Fisher and his fellow developers incorporated the island as "Miami Beach," with its own government structure and public buildings. He envisioned a self-sufficient city to serve every need and desire of its temporary and permanent residents.

When he arrived in Miami, Fisher brought with him the one thing that was needed to make his dream a reality—plenty of cash. His sale of the Prest-O-Lite company gave him a nest egg of some $5 million, which he used to purchase land and begin the process of dredging sand from the Atlantic Ocean to expand his property.

Even as Fisher's early attempts to draw new investors and settlers failed, he remained committed to the idea of Miami Beach. Realizing that luxury hotels would draw customers for his developments, he offered six hundred feet of prime beachfront to any investor willing to build a $100,000 hotel. There were no takers. Just before the outbreak of World War I, he built the Lincoln Hotel, a modest hotel with just thirty-five rooms. He continued to invest in the necessary infrastructure to support his new city and in the attractions that would draw visitors. In 1919, tired of the on-again, off-again service of the Miami Electric Light & Power Company, he incorporated the Miami Beach Electric Company, with its own power plant, to deliver economical and reliable power. The same year, he and his fellow developers on the island organized a streetcar company—a persistent money loser—to bring visitors and potential customers to Miami Beach. Two years later, they tried to sell the line to the City of Miami without success.

To bolster the image of Miami Beach, Fisher sold his home on Miami's Brickell Avenue, the most prestigious address in the city, and built a $65,000 mansion in Miami Beach on Lincoln Road (later Collins Avenue). He used his home to entertain prospective investors and his cronies; it remained isolated from the mainstream of Miami society until after the war. His wife, Jane, recalled the move as initially living like a pioneer where everything had to be brought in by boat or truck. The ramshackle Collins Bridge (1913) was eventually supplemented in 1920 by a causeway (now MacArthur Causeway) and then dismantled entirely and replaced by the Venetian Causeway in 1926.

During World War I, Fisher rented his polo grounds to the federal government for use as training fields for new pilots. The rent was one dollar a year, but his competitors complained that his generous concession had underlying motives of self-aggrandizement. To some extent, this was true. Officers and enlisted men who were stationed at Miami Beach became convinced that it was truly a paradise, and they wrote home about this little slice of heaven. After the war, many of them returned to visit and buy.

VENETIAN WAY, CONNECTING MIAMI AND MIAMI BEACH, FLORIDA

Top: The Collins Bridge, a ramshackle wooden structure built in 1913 between the mainland and Miami Beach, was replaced in 1920 by a modern causeway, which stretched for three and a half miles. *Courtesy of the Florida Historical Society.*

Bottom: The Venetian Causeway, built in 1926, provided an elegant and modern connection between Miami Beach and the mainland. It replaced the old Collins Bridge, which was dismantled. *Courtesy of the Florida Historical Society.*

Prior to 1920, Fisher had sought to duplicate the appeal of Palm Beach for the mega-wealthy of America, but his efforts in this direction were woefully unsuccessful. The sedate advertising he used was designed to fit his view of what the Newport and Palm Beach crowds might find attractive. This was a remarkable change from the full-bore, often garish advertising techniques he used to promote his racetrack and other activities. Instead of innovating and giving free rein to his own imagination, he laced himself in a straightjacket of conservatism, and it showed. Mark S. Foster, the author of Fisher's biography *Castles in the Sand*, described the failure of his prewar efforts to attract visitors, investors and families to his development as discouraging. "At times," Foster wrote, "he could not even *give* property away." Not even his offers to finance the construction of new homes met with success. It looked like Miami Beach would be a bust.

His competitors on the island took a different tack, however, and advertised Miami Beach as a "fun" location. Not until the postwar years did Fisher adopt this viewpoint, but he finally decided that real success in selling Miami Beach would not come from convincing members of the "old wealth" families to buy property; instead, it rested with the new generation of "auto" magnates, manufacturers and the growing affluent middle class. These were the people with whom he was most familiar and whom he understood. Soon, many of the "gasoline millionaires," men like Harvey Firestone, Harvey Stutz, Albert Champion, Edsel Ford and Frank Seiberling, bought land and built lavish homes along Collins Avenue.

Once he clearly identified his target market, Fisher set the tone and the direction the new community would take. With the advent of the Roaring Twenties and the on-the-go attitude of younger Americans, he was determined that Miami Beach would capture the spirit of the era and project the image of never-ending fun. Carl Fisher aimed his community as a "vacation paradise," a mixture of permanent homes and luxury hotels where visitors and residents could take advantage of polo fields, golf courses, beaches, nightclubs, fishing, high-speed boat racing and casinos.

The American experience with German submarine warfare and the ill-fated voyages of the *Titanic* and *Lusitania* dampened enthusiasm for overseas cruising, while the social and economic dislocation caused by the war cast a pall on the idea of a European vacation. The war, which had fueled American industry, also left a burgeoning middle class that had extra money to spend. To ensure that Americans had the proper perspective of the high life in Miami Beach, Fisher spent hundreds of thousands of dollars advertising the pleasures of Miami Beach. Of all the Florida promoters, only George Merrick would spend more than he did.

Of all the activities offered at his Miami Beach properties, Fisher spent the most money on polo. Determined to demonstrate that his developments rivaled ritzy Palm Beach, he concentrated on making them the center of polo, long considered the "sport of kings." The first polo match in Miami Beach took place on February 20, 1919, at Fisher's Flamingo Polo Grounds.

The Miami Beach casino was the center of life in Miami Beach. Here residents could gather to spend time on the beach, swim in a large freshwater pool, eat, play tennis or simply visit with other tourists and residents. *Courtesy of the Florida Historical Society.*

When he first starting developing Miami Beach, Carl Fisher wanted to attract the same clientele as ritzy Palm Beach. He spent more than $2 million by 1923 on making his new town the epicenter of the sport of polo, which was often referred to as the "sport of kings." *Courtesy of the Florida Historical Society.*

A City from Whole Cloth

According to biographer Mark Foster, one of Fisher's associates estimated that he had spent more than $2 million on the sport by 1923. Always a competitive person, he learned to ride just so he could participate in the game.

Fisher, one of the original owners of the Indianapolis Motor Speedway, was a fanatic about any machine that was fast. His love for speed fit nicely with the proximity of the Atlantic Ocean, and in 1915, he sponsored the first powerboat regatta in Miami. For the next several years, Fisher, in partnership with the American Power Boat Association, created a series of regattas that offered substantial monetary prizes, including the $5,000 Wood-Fisher Trophy. He called on his friends in the automobile and airplane industries to contribute additional prizes, as well as technical support for improved engines. Championship racer and boat designer Garfield A. "Gar" Wood, a friend of many years, credited him with being a major force behind the development of fast racing boats. In the October 1925 edition of *American Motorist*, Wood paid homage once again to Fisher for bringing "Florida and Miami beach more national prominence" than ever when he bought a fleet of eleven small runabouts, powered by one-hundred-horsepower marine engines and driven by nationally known race car drivers, to compete in a race that depended on skill. According to Wood, it provided "real competition, all of the boats being exactly the same mold and all the engines producing the same speed, there being less than one second's difference in the speed of the fastest and slowest of the eleven boats." For Fisher, powerboat races added to the allure of Miami Beach as a sunny playground because the race "gave the crowds which thronged the shores of Biscayne Bay a real thrill and interested thousands in boats because they were able to see what could be done with the small craft."

What he did for sanctioned racing, he also did for the rumrunners who plied the route between the Bahamas and Florida. Prohibition agents determined to enforce the ban of liquor smuggled between the islands and the Sunshine State found that they faced an uphill struggle to keep up with the technological changes that generally kept the boats of the smugglers out of their snares. For Fisher, who hated Prohibition, providing expert advice and state-of-the-art equipment became just another way he could frustrate the enforcement of this odious law. Gar Wood alluded to Fisher's assistance in developing "the runabout and cruiser, which are utility craft and adaptable to the uses of the man who enjoys both a boat for pleasure and commercial purposes...across the Gulf Stream to Bimini Island, Havana, and Key West." Powerboat racing allowed him to indulge in a sport he considered exciting, but the bottom line was that it added to the mystique and exciting image of Miami Beach.

Tennis was another sport that Fisher promoted in Miami Beach. An enthusiastic though relatively unskilled player, he realized that other Americans, fascinated by the game, wanted to play, and he included a number of tennis courts in all of his development plans. In addition to sponsoring tournaments that brought in the best amateur and professional players in the world—William "Big Bill" Tilden, his doubles partner Vincent Richards, Helen Wills (Moody) and Suzanne Lenglen—he provided free lodging for them to stay and fraternize with paying guests at his hotels. For a few guests willing to pay for the privilege, private lessons with these stars could be arranged. Just as he did with other sports, Fisher considered any investments he made to be just the cost of doing business in glamorous Miami Beach.

Although not an avid golfer, Fisher was aware that this was the one sport that appealed more than any other to visitors to the Sunshine State, and he vigorously promoted it as well. By 1925, three private courses, including an eighteen-hole course at Fisher's Miami Beach Country Club, were available for play.

The City of Miami and the City of Hialeah offered municipal courses, while Merrick created the course in front of the Biltmore Hotel, the Coral Gables Golf Club. It was remarkable that Fisher, who had little aptitude for the game, nevertheless saw its value as a magnet to draw the rich and powerful to Miami Beach. James M. Cox, governor of Ohio and Democratic presidential nominee in 1920, and other politicians and business moguls joined the likes of Babe Ruth, Will Rogers, Jack Dempsey, Gene Tunney and countless movie stars in playing with the top amateur and professional golfers of the day. Always seeking to arouse more interest in the game (and to attract more patrons to his hotels), Fisher presented unusual golfing spectacles such as "archery" golf. Other Fisher-inspired golf events pitted skilled players in other sports—jai alai, tennis, baseball—against talented golfers. Even zoo animals were used as caddies in publicity matches, and Rosie the elephant proved to be an instant hit with the public.

The same Florida sunshine that made the beach resorts so popular also made golf a year-round sport on the peninsula. "Sir" Walter Hagen, Gene Sarazen, Leo Diegel, Johnny Farrell and MacDonald Smith were among the most popular professional golfers to play Fisher's courses on Miami Beach, and they also played other courses around the state. Bobby Jones, the most famous amateur player in the world, frequently joined his professional colleagues in tournaments and exhibitions.

Although golf was just one of the many entertainments Fisher offered in Miami Beach, the golf craze swept the nation and the rest of Florida. From

Although he was not an aficionado of the game, Fisher knew that golf was the postwar American sensation, and he included several courses in his Miami Beach development. This picture shows the putting greens in front of his Flamingo Hotel on Miami Beach, although the caption on the picture states that it was in Miami. Miami Beach and the city of Miami were often referred to as the same place. *Courtesy of the Florida Historical Society.*

Carl Fisher enjoyed welcoming his friends on the golf course with Rosie, the elephant that would caddy the round. Rosie was an instant hit with the public and was used in other publicity stunts. *Courtesy of the Moorhead Collection.*

the simple two-hole course built by Colonel J. Hamilton Gillespie in the yard of his Sarasota home in 1886, virtually every established town and city in the Sunshine State boasted a course. Soon, entire communities dedicated to the sport rose from the flat Florida plains to surround courses designed by such golfing luminaries as Donald J. Ross, A.W. Tillinghast, William Langford, Seth Raynor, Herbert Strong and John Duncan Dunn. By 1925, Florida counted more than 150 courses open to golfers of all skill levels.

In 1924, Fisher used a plot made up of more than two million cubic yards of sand dredged from Biscayne Bay to create La Gorce Country Club, named in honor of his friend Rockwell La Gorce. In 1928, despite the declining economy of South Florida and the bust, he hosted the first La Gorce Open Golf Tournament with a purse of $15,000 to boost sagging property sales and decreasing tourist revenues. Despite its claim to be "the biggest money golf tournament" ever and the participation of the most famous professionals of the era, the open had a minimal impact on land sales. The simple fact was that the boom in Florida land was over, not to be revived until the 1960s.

What Fisher pioneered, other promoters copied. To ensure that the public knew about the hoopla surrounding the activities in Miami Beach, he employed a staff of publicity agents who made sure that newspapers and magazines received articles, pictures and other interesting tidbits. The classic Carl Fisher story about his quest for publicity came when, immediately after a strenuous game of polo, his friend, Julius Fleischmann, died of a heart attack. Although upset, he took the time to remind one of his publicity men that any reports of the tragedy in the nation's newspapers should bear the dateline of Miami Beach. Everything provided grist for the Fisher publicity mill. Polly Redford, in *Billion Dollar Sandbar: A Biography of Miami Beach*, quotes Carl's ex-wife Jane on how the scantily clad bathing beauty (by the standards of the 1920s) became the symbol of Miami Beach:

> *It was at the Roman Pools* [a bathing pavilion on Miami Beach owned by Fisher] *that Jane caused a scandal by appearing without the long black stockings that were standard swimming attire at the time. She claimed that this is how bathing beauties began on the Beach. For when a Miami minister used her bare knees as a living example of the depravity of Modern Woman, Carl said, "By God, Jane, you've started something! Why, dammit, I've been trying for months to think up an idea for advertising the Beach. We'll get the prettiest girls we can find and put them in the goddamndest tightest and shortest bathing suits and no stockings or swim shoes either. We'll have their pictures taken and send them all over the goddamn country."*

The Flamingo Hotel, Carl Fisher's grand hotel on Miami Beach, offered guests the latest amenities, sports and the opportunity to moor their yachts at the hotel's docks. Efforts to transplant a flock of exotic African pink flamingos on the grounds of the hotel met with only marginal success. *Courtesy of the Florida Historical Society.*

The modest swimsuits of the 1920s cannot compare in any way with the thongs and topless bikinis of today's bathing beauties, but the movement from the demure top-to-bottom attire of the earlier 1900s created a sensation. Nothing guaranteed more attention than "half-dressed" women, and nothing promised more fun than the prospect of cavorting with them under the Florida sun.

Fisher poured more than $100,000 a year in promoting Miami Beach and considered it money well spent. Still, Fisher argued that his publicity efforts, which certainly stressed Miami Beach, produced results for all developments in the Miami area, and he proposed the creation of a single agency, with staffers paid by a consortium of developers, to handle marketing for them. Such a joint effort would be cost effective by reducing any duplication of efforts. Although his proposal received little backing at the local level, it did produce some limited results nationally when magazines and newspapers commissioned articles about the boom.

According to T.G. Weigall, George Merrick outdid Fisher in generating publicity for his Coral Gables development and employed a publicity staff that kept mimeograph and teletype machines operating twenty-four hours a day spitting out "news" to the nation's media. In 1925, the *Miami Herald*

Contractors
and Builders!

The building boom reached such a frenzy by 1925 that developers found it difficult to attract and employ enough contractors to complete projected buildings. Often they placed advertisements in major magazines urging contractors to come south—with their laborers. *Courtesy of the Florida Historical Society.*

bragged about being the largest newspaper in the world when it produced an edition consisting of twenty-two sections and 504 pages, most of which were advertisements for Coral Gables, Miami Beach, Hialeah/Opa-locka and other smaller developments.

In addition to spending vast sums advertising Miami Beach, Fisher continued to invest heavily in hotels and land. Although he owned the small Lincoln Hotel—which he warned guests in advance was an ordinary and unpretentious little establishment—he realized that other more elegant lodgings were required for the thousands of winter visitors, all of whom were potential customers for his residential developments. In 1919, he announced the construction of the magnificent 200-room Flamingo Hotel at the astronomical cost of $1.5 million. By 1921, the demand for rooms had exceeded the capacity of the hotel, and Fisher decided that more hotels were needed. Since no other investor would step forward, he announced the construction of three new hotels over the next three years—the 189-room Nautilus (1923); the King Cole (1924); and the Boulevard (1925). Within two years, however, other investors decided the market was ripe for more hotels. Arthur Pancoast opened the 110-room Pancoast Hotel in 1923, followed by J. Perry Stoltz's Fleetwood Hotel in 1924. Newton Baker Taylor Roney announced plans for his $2 million Roney Plaza in 1924 and opened it in 1926, just in time for the devastating hurricane that year. By 1925, Miami Beach counted 4,000 available rooms spread among fifty-six hotels, in addition to nearly two hundred apartment buildings offering longer-term rentals. Enough? Not

President-elect Warren G. Harding was an inveterate golfer and, so the rumors went, a social drinker. When Carl Fisher persuaded him to come to Miami Beach in 1921 for a few rounds of golf and some good liquor, he came. His visit proved to be decisive in boosting sales on the beach. *Courtesy of the Moorhead Collection.*

quite. The October and November 1925 *American Motorist* magazines carried advertisements from the Miami Beach Chamber of Commerce seeking contractors and builders to build an additional one hundred hotels and three hundred more apartment buildings. "New Hotels and Apartments are being erected, but not half enough to accommodate the people flocking here. There is work for everybody in the building line and contractors are urged to bring their workers here with them."

The investments Carl Fisher made in hotels, golf courses, polo grounds and other assorted entertainment/activity amenities were secondary to his major goal of improving the value of his real estate. Although he originally purchased his Miami Beach property in 1913, it took him almost eight years to realize any kind of profit. In 1920, for example, sales of Fisher properties totaled only about $500,000, and as late as the 1921–22 winter season, he was forced to borrow money just to pay the quarterly installment of his income tax. He was, to put it bluntly, land rich and cash poor.

In January 1921, Fisher persuaded President-elect Warren G. Harding and his wife to spend a few days playing golf in Miami Beach. Although a frequent visitor to Florida (he had in-laws in Rockledge), this was his first trip to the Sunshine State as the next president of the United States. Whether or not the attendant press coverage, augmented by the contributions of Fisher's own publicity agents, made the visit decisive in boosting land sales, Harding's Miami Beach visit dominated the front pages of the nation's newspapers and directed the attention of the American public on this small spit of Atlantic coastline. Perhaps engaging in hyperbole, Fisher alleged that his company showed a profit for that season of "about $9,000,000." It is doubtful, however, that this was true, since this was the year he was forced to borrow money to pay his taxes.

Within a year, the "boom" kicked in and Fisher's fortunes changed dramatically. Although it is difficult to find absolutely reliable figures—given the hype and exaggeration that accompanied newspaper reports of the period—1923 land sales reached $6 million for Fisher properties alone in Miami Beach, followed in 1924 by an additional $8 million. At the peak of the boom in 1925, his companies reported some $23 million in sales. The boom spread across the Sunshine State, and developers, many of whom had started with little or nothing in their wallets a year or so before, now tossed about similar sums with an air of complete indifference. "Estimates of his fortune at the peak of the boom ranged from $50 million up to $100 million," Mark Foster wrote. "Nobody really knew, including Fisher. He had very little liquidity. His fortune was mostly on paper, and he was a lousy record keeper."

CHAPTER 7
George Edgar Merrick

Mr. Merrick was passionately in love with Florida; and to me, he always seemed to believe in Florida in quite a different way from that of most of the other "developers" that I encountered there. He loved Florida for its own sake, and not for the money that could be made out of its exploitation; he saw in Florida the last outpost of the United States, a fresh and unspoiled territory which it would be criminal to let develop along haphazard, ugly, or unscientific lines.

—T.H. Weigall, Boom in Paradise, *1926*

What Carl Fisher was doing in Miami Beach with his own money inspired a number of imitators, some more successful than others. One of the most innovative and remarkable men of the boom was George E. Merrick, who parlayed a small 160-acre family farm into a planned development of 3,000 acres. Although some historians like to portray him as a "rags-to-riches" phenomenon, the reality is that Merrick was the product of a solid middle-class environment, the son of a Yale graduate and himself a graduate of Rollins College. He also attended Columbia University in New York in pursuit of degrees in law and literature. Unlike his major rivals—Carl Fisher, who grew up without a father in his mother's boarding home, and David P. Davis, who never graduated from high school—George's upbringing was stable.

George returned to the Miami area upon his father's death in 1911 to manage the family farm, Coral Gables. Married to Eunice Peacock, the daughter of Coconut Grove pioneer Alfred Peacock, in 1916, he set about acquiring more acreage and making what he now called the plantation into a profitable business venture. Eunice brought a considerable dowry of land to the marriage, and by 1920, Merrick had expanded his holdings to more than one thousand acres and operated the largest fruit and vegetable farm in South Florida. Eventually, his holdings would amount to more than ten thousand acres.

Soon after his marriage to Eunice, Merrick began to plan to convert his agricultural lands into a large planned development for year-round residents. The success of Palm Beach in drawing wealthy winter residents and the much-ballyhooed plans of Carl Fisher in Miami Beach convinced him that such a project was economically feasible. Unlike Palm Beach, with its hotel/spa emphasis, and Miami Beach, with its projected seasonal residencies, his planned community would concentrate on attracting a permanent population of middle-class retirees and young families. The only ingredient missing to make his dream a reality was money.

When George presented his idea of a planned Coral Gables community to bankers in Miami in the hopes of securing their financial backing before the war, none of them was interested. Since few of them believed that that "damned fool" Carl Fisher could make his development of Miami Beach pay off—and using his own money at that—why should they risk investing their funds in turning a truck farm into houses? No, they reasoned, George E. Merrick should stick to what he does best, and that was to farm. Far from being discouraged, he decided to set up a real estate office in Miami to learn the business of selling land from the ground up and gradually accumulate enough money to make his dream a reality. A personable and educated individual, Merrick was a quick learner whose enthusiasm and integrity made him successful. In staid prewar Miami, his family connections, enhanced by his marriage to Eunice, also helped.

By 1920, the atmosphere had changed dramatically. Large amounts of money—more than ever before—were in circulation in the United States, the automobile was supreme as a cultural symbol and an eager public, weary of war, was ready to spend the money accumulated during the industrial expansion fueled by the war. What could not be purchased outright could be had on the ubiquitous installment plan that dominated consumer spending. Americans were ready to spend and spend big. Prohibition, the new Jazz Age and the end of the Victorian era, exemplified by the infamous "flapper girls," signaled the beginning of the Roaring Twenties and the age of truly conspicuous consumption. Fisher's Miami Beach lots had started to sell, and everyone in the nation knew that Miami was "America's playground."

George Edgar Merrick

Merrick benefitted from the hoopla created by Fisher in Miami Beach, Mizner in Palm Beach and D.P. Davis, who had invested the money he made operating food stands in Jacksonville during the war in a large Miami subdivision, Shadowlawn. Although George's reputation as a businessman was very good, the bankers he approached to fund his proposed development were still reluctant to lend him large sums, since Coral Gables was inland and far removed from the beach. Nevertheless, he continued to look for other sources of funding and soon made connections with several large insurance companies that were willing to take a chance. Unlike the locals, the idea that waterfront property was essential to any successful development did not figure in their assessments of his chances. With financing arranged, Merrick plunged ahead.

To ensure that his new community met the highest standards of the City Beautiful movement that was in vogue during the first decades of the twentieth century, he hired Phineas E. Paist, a Philadelphia architect who had worked as part of the design team for James Deering's Vizcaya mansion, to create a central architectural theme and to ensure that all homes constructed in Coral Gables conformed to these standards. Paist, who would later design the "Florida home" for the 1937 World's Fair exhibit, was joined by artist Denman Fink, Merrick's uncle, and Frank Button, the designer of Chicago's Lincoln Park, in creating an environment that blended colorful tropical plants, broad streets, canals and Mediterranean Revival architecture into an integrated whole. New arrivals got an early view of the architecture of Coral Gables when they entered the development through the massive Douglas Road coquina arch, built at a cost of $1 million, which spanned the road. A collaboration of Paist and Fink, it was a work of beauty, and soon other smaller subdivisions throughout the Sunshine State featured versions of the arch. Most lacked the scale and symmetry of the Gables' arch, but it had become such a symbol of Florida's land boom that few developers could resist the urge to copy it.

Unlike Fisher's Miami Beach, which was created from ocean sand, Coral Gables presented Merrick and his design team with a solid, though depressingly flat, platform on which they could let their imaginations run wild. Starting from scratch, Merrick made use of the few natural features to enhance his development. Other features were created through the ingenious use of dirt dredged from the many canals, many featuring gondolas, that crisscrossed Coral Gables. An old coquina quarry provided an opportunity to create a community swimming pool (1924). Known as the Venetian Pool, it

The Venetian Pool in Coral Gables, built on the site of a limestone quarry, was touted as the most beautiful pool in the United States. It became the symbol of Merrick's Coral Gables development. *Courtesy of the Florida Historical Society.*

All public buildings in Coral Gables conformed to the overall Mediterranean Revival theme. The Coral Gables High School building shows how a determined architect could bring style and panache to the design of a public institution. *Courtesy of the Florida Historical Society.*

was soon featured in various advertisements as the largest and most beautiful pool in the United States.

The first lot sold in Coral Gables was purchased on November 27, 1921, even before the first roads and infrastructure were completed. Edward E. "Doc" Dammers, who had been selling land in Miami since 1910, was hired to head the sales staff. Part charlatan and 100 percent character, Dammers began selling lots in Coral Gables from the back of a wagon, frequently using giveaways of knickknacks and geegaws to attract customers. Within a few months, Merrick purchased a fleet of seventy-six buses to bring in potential customers. From as far away as Atlanta, Montgomery and even New York, Chicago and San Francisco, "prospects" were given a free ride, accommodations, food and a "royal time" in exchange for seeing Coral Gables and listening to sales pitches. (This technique is still used by real estate salespersons today as they offer raw land, condominiums and time-shares to the public.) Merrick's innovative way of finding customers was quickly duplicated by other developers, although on a smaller scale, and Florida-bound buses were a common sight on the nation's new highways. Despite the fact that some of the people who took advantage of these free mini-vacations were "lookie-loos" without the means of paying for any purchase, there were enough bona fide buyers to justify the expense.

In the master plan for Coral Gables, large community areas—golf courses, tennis courts, bridle paths, hotels—were set aside. Standardized curbing, sidewalks and lampposts lined broad roadways. Between 1921 and 1925, fifteen hundred houses were built, two hundred miles of roadway were graded and paved and eighty miles of sidewalks provided ready access to every area of the development. The Coral Gables Country Club, presided over by Henry Dutton, featured an open dance pavilion, with colored lights strung from ornamental bushes, in addition to the course. A fire station, water plant, administration building and power plant completed the basic structures. After the City of Coral Gables was incorporated in 1925, Paist also designed a city hall that opened in 1928. (Much later, in 1939, he also designed the Coral Gables Police and Fire Station, which reflected the overall theme Merrick had established years before.)

There was a lot going on in Coral Gables during the first half of the decade of the 1920s. Visitors could stay at the luxurious Casa Loma Hotel, stroll through neatly manicured parks, take a gondola ride along the miles of canals, play golf at two country clubs or partake in a variety of other activities. Prospective buyers could also take in a twice-a-day lecture by

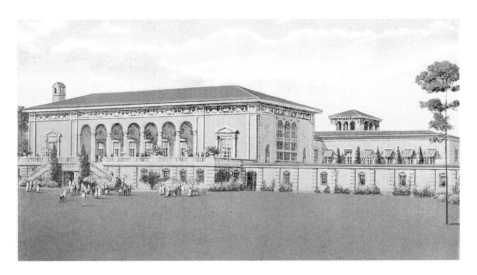

The Coral Gables Country Club featured an open dance pavilion. Presided over by Henry Dutton, who was the recreation director for the development, it quickly became an exclusive venue for famous personalities and wealthy residents. *Courtesy of the Florida Historical Society.*

three-time presidential candidate William Jennings Bryan. Never a winner, Bryan nevertheless remained a popular figure, and his persuasive rhetoric was as much public spectacle as convincing sales pitch. (Bryan, who once said, "Nobody ever made a million dollars honestly," died in 1925. His estate was well in excess of that amount, most of it in real estate.)

In mid-1925, John McEntee Bowman, who headed the Miami Biltmore Group, announced the construction of a new $10 million hotel that would feature not one but two additional eighteen-hole golf courses designed by the most famous of all golf course designers, Donald J. Ross. When it opened in January 1926, the Miami-Biltmore became *the* destination for America's beautiful people. Popular dance bands provided the background music for crowds of well-known personalities and countless hangers-on. Coral Gables truly was the "Miami Riviera."

The first sections of houses in Coral Gables were built in the prevailing Mediterranean Revival style popularized by Addison Mizner in Palm Beach. Color schemes, architectural details and landscaping had to pass muster with the Board of Architects Review Panel, created by Paist (and still operating today), before any actual construction could take place. Conformity to Merrick's overall plan was the order of the day, and Paist, Fink and Button were the men who enforced it. Proposed buildings that

The Miami-Biltmore became the "in" destination of America's celebrities. Two Donald J. Ross–designed golf courses provided a championship venue for the noted golfers of the day. *Courtesy of the Florida Historical Society.*

did not adhere to the standards of his master plan were rejected out of hand, and no compromises were made.

In August 1925, Merrick changed the overall plan for Coral Gables somewhat when he signed a deal for one thousand new homes to be built by the American Building Corporation of Cincinnati. This $75 million purchase was the largest order for new homes recorded up to that time. Utilizing a team of twelve architects, he designated fourteen new areas of the development to feature homes from specific international regions of the world—Persia, South Africa, China, France and Italy. Many of these "Village" homes carried a projected price tag of $100,000 or more. About one hundred of these "regional" homes were built before the hurricane of 1926. While built according to the highest architectural standards mandated by the Architects Review Panel, today they provide a beautiful but discordant element to Coral Gables. Author T.H. Weigall, who worked in Merrick's Publicity Department in 1925, described the results thusly:

> *The Moorish watch-towers and the red roofs of Coral Gables were inclined to be more than a little overwhelming; and although in that city alone there were nearly a dozen areas confined to different architectural styles, they were so large in themselves that the effect of variation from any one standpoint was generally lost.*

The same month Merrick agreed to the deal with the American Building Corporation, he paid $2.5 million for the 160-acre Le Jeune citrus grove, divided it into housing lots and then put them up for sale. In just twenty-four hours, Merrick's salesmen recorded contracts worth $5,555,850. Under the direction of "Doc" Dammers, chief salesman and mayor of the newly incorporated city of Coral Gables, a sales force of three thousand sold contracts for almost $98,000,000 for the year—most with small down payments of 25 percent and a promissory note for the balance to be paid in three annual installments. William Jennings Bryan gave the sales force inspirational talks to stimulate it to make even more sales. There were more than twenty thousand vacant lots in the development by the middle of 1926, and during the summer of that year, Merrick sent a mailer to all owners urging them to begin construction on their homes.

In the October 1925 volume of *American Motorist*, an advertisement for Coral Gables bearing the name George E. Merrick touted the value of land in the "Miami Riviera" as a good investment. "Coral Gables property," it

Unique Chinese Village, Coral Gables, Florida   182

In 1925, Merrick designated fourteen areas of Coral Gables that would feature homes from different international regions. Although some people argued that the inclusion of such homes disrupted the architectural purity of Coral Gables, his decision stood. Only about one hundred of the homes were built before the bust hit in late 1926. This picture shows homes for the "Chinese Village" section of Coral Gables. *Courtesy of the Florida Historical Society*.

proclaimed, "has been steadily rising in value. Some of it has shown a 100 per cent increase *every year*." It also promised that purchasers could look forward to the completion "within a few years" of the

> *$15,000,000 University of Miami, the $500,000 Mahi temple of the Mystic Shrine, a $1,000,000 University High School, a $150,000 Railway Station, a Military Academy and Stadium, a Theatre, the College for Young Women of the Sisters of Saint Joseph, a magnificent Conservatory of Music, and other remarkable projects.*

Grand plans for sure, but 1925 marked the height of the Florida boom, and no one even considered such plans to be out of the realm of probability.

There were heavy costs associated with the development of Coral Gables. Estimates by various historians of the total investment dollars Merrick put into the project between 1921 and 1926 range between $100 million and $150 million. Estimates of how much money he made range between $50 million and $100 million. In 1935, *Time* magazine, reporting on a Securities Exchange Commission investigation of the

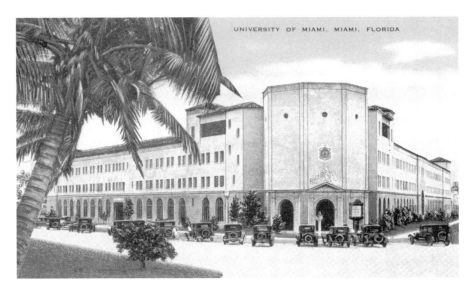

One of George Merrick's most enduring legacies is the University of Miami, which he established to add an important cultural aspect to his development. It opened in 1926, just in time for the hurricane of that year. The nickname the students of the university chose was "the Hurricanes." *Courtesy of the Florida Historical Society.*

operations of Merrick's Coral Gables Corporation, estimated its weekly payroll obligation at $200,000 a week. Advertising and publicity costs were $4 million per year.

Despite the burden of continuing to finance expansion and development, George Merrick, like all promoters and developers in Florida in 1925 and early 1926, felt there was no end in sight for the land boom. There was only one way to go, they thought, and that was up!

CHAPTER 8

David P. Davis

THE ISLAND MAKER

Not alone the thrill of tropical moonlight stealing through the leaves of swaying palm trees and dancing about like diamonds on the bosom of the bay, but a veritable Venice at one's home-door for those who live on Davis Islands…Here are ceaselessly moving waters, ever lapping the foundation of Davis Islands domiciles. Here, too, are the picturesque gondolas and other sorts of craft moored to fantastically colored poles—right at one's door-step—ready for the moonlight sail to the accompaniment of music which steals across the bay.
—*D.P. Davis Properties, Inc., sales brochure, 1924*

On October 24, 1925, David P. "Doc" Davis placed an advertisement in the *Tampa Tribune* and other media outlets that all the lots in his Davis Islands development had been sold for $18,138,000. An additional $8,250,000, so the ad read, would be returned to would-be purchasers because there was nothing left to sell. Barely a year since the first three hundred lots had been offered for sale in 1924, Davis was on top of the world. His initial investment of approximately $5,000,000 produced a paper profit of almost 400 percent. Everything had gone right in the past, so what in the world could go wrong in the future?

Unlike many of the promoters of the land boom, David Paul Davis was a homegrown product of the Sunshine State. The son of an itinerant engineman on Florida riverboats, he was born in Green Cove Springs—although several biographers have mistakenly asserted that he was born in Tampa—and lived in a number of different Florida towns; Tampa was

David P. "Doc" Davis had a dream of an all-new and different development at the mouth of the Hillsborough River on tidal islands in Tampa Bay. He used the same methods of dredging new soil from the bottom of the bay to create larger, higher islands that Carl Fisher had pioneered in Miami Beach. In 1924, there was nothing much to see on the islands, but he sold out his initial offering of lots and development proceeded. *Courtesy of the Florida Historical Society*.

only one of them. He attended public schools in Tampa, but he never graduated. As a young man, he worked in a variety of different jobs, none of which paid much money. In 1905, at age twenty, he left Florida for Panama to work on the canal that was under construction there. In 1915, he returned to the Sunshine State and took up residency in Jacksonville. There he met and married Marjorie H. Merritt. With the outbreak of World War I, he operated a ferry between Jacksonville and Camp Johnston, which the military constructed across the St. Johns River from the city. He also secured the franchise to operate a canteen on the post. By the time the Armistice ended the war in 1918, Davis had amassed a small fortune from his canteen operations. He decided to take his family (and his money) to Miami, where Carl Fisher was making noises with his Miami Beach operations and where smaller promoters were hawking residential lots with less prestigious addresses.

David P. Davis

Starting small, Davis persuaded the owner of a small subdivision of four hundred lots, known as the Railroad Shops addition in the Buena Vista section of Miami, to allow D.P. Davis, Inc., to sell the lots for him. Although the property had languished in the market for several years, Davis was willing to bet that he could sell the lots and sell them quickly. With nothing to lose, the owner agreed to his proposal. After doubling the asking price for individual lots, Davis invested $1,000 of his own funds in advertising them. Within days, the lots were sold, netting him a commission of $40,000. Only a few days after he liquidated these lots and collected his earnings, Davis invested $47,000 in the Alta Vista subdivision. Within forty days, he sold them out, converting his original investment into a substantial $150,000. This became the formula he followed for the rest of his business life—invest a little, sell for a lot, take the profits and invest again.

Davis operated two real estate companies in Miami during this period. His D.P. Davis, Inc., company purchased raw land and developed it, while his United Realty Company handled commercial developments. In early 1920, Davis entered into the most significant deal of his business life. He purchased a seventy-two-acre plot of ground in the Buena Vista section of Miami for $175,000. On July 1, 1920, he put thirty-two acres, now called the Shadowlawn subdivision, on sale. Although he decided to place properties on the market outside the traditional "snowbird" winter season, it was a huge success, and the entire offering sold out for $396,000. Davis's reputation as one of the most important promoters of Florida real estate was firmly established. Michael J. Boonstra, whose master's thesis traced Davis's life, quotes him as saying that after this bit of success, his career was "smooth sailing." Perhaps so, but not for long.

Although most initial buyers in Shadowlawn purchased properties with the clear intention of reselling them and clearing a profit, Davis realized that construction of homes on the vacant lots would immensely improve their value. In order to encourage those who bought lots to build homes, he started to lend money for this purpose. The November 1922 issue of the *Home Designer* featured the model homes he offered in Shadowlawn—an eclectic mixture of Mission, Pueblo Revival and even English Colonial styles. He quickly followed this success by opening the Biltmore subdivision in the Buena Vista section. Focusing on creating a viable business district for the homeowners in Biltmore, he spent $20,000 to build a post office, which he leased to the federal government. Soon, other investors followed his lead, and a small, but stylish, commercial center, with broad sidewalks and city lighting, developed. The Moore Furniture Company, rated as the "second finest furniture store" in the country, was the linchpin of this development. Buyers came from all of the new developments in the Miami area—Coral Gables, Miami Beach, Hialeah and others—to buy at Moore's. A 1926 advertisement noted:

> *It is one of the largest and most completely equipped furniture stores in the South. Situated on the Dixie [Highway], as one enters Miami, it strikes the keynote of progress and prosperity to be encountered everywhere in Miami's industrial enterprises.*

Success in Miami meant that Davis attracted attention from other men who sought to interest him in developing properties outside the city. In late 1922 or early 1923, he was introduced to Alfred Roy Trafford of Cocoa. Trafford, who made almost daily train runs from Cocoa to Miami selling property, convinced Davis to visit the Brevard County area. Impressed with the area's potential for development, Davis purchased one hundred acres of land on the north side of Cocoa and announced that he and his brother, Milton, would develop Carleton Terrace. Promising to spend more than $100,000 on infrastructure, public parks and landscaping, he set about clearing and grading the property. On January 28, 1924, the first of the deed-restricted lots—all new houses had to have a minimum value of $3,500; no stables, hog pens or outhouses could be built; and no house could be sold, leased or rented to non-Caucasians—went on sale. Two months later, total lot sales exceeded $200,000. By December 1925, all lots had been sold and housing construction was well underway.

According to one estimate, Davis accumulated more than $5 million in profits between 1921 and 1924 from his dealings in Miami and Cocoa real estate, but such wealth was not enough for him. In Miami, Carl Fisher and George Merrick were regarded as the premier builders, followed by Glenn Curtiss in Opa-locka, Hialeah and Miami Springs. Davis was an important figure, but running a distant fourth or fifth was not enough to satisfy his ego. In Cocoa, he was the undisputed king of real estate, but with a population of only two thousand, Cocoa was a small kingdom. He looked around for a place where he could be the kingfish, and he found just the place in Tampa.

The Tampa area, like most areas of Florida, was claiming a share of the boom. To the northeast, the old Bertha Palmer property of Temple Terrace, controlled by two related companies—Temple Terrace Estates, Inc., and Temple Terraces, Inc.—emerged as the leading development.

David P. Davis

Temple Terrace Estates, Inc., marketed the area as a residential development surrounding a Tom Bendelow–designed golf course, while Temple Terraces, Inc., managed the orange groves that were attached to each residential lot. The marketing advertisements for the development stressed days filled with golf; quiet, idyllic afternoons spent tending orange trees; and delightful evenings spent dining with fellow golfers in the country club. In fact, meals at the country club were such an integral part of the Temple Terrace lifestyle that very few homes were built with kitchens.

In 1922, D. Collins Gillette, Burks L. Hamner and Maude Fowler pooled their resources to make Temple Terrace a reality. Broad streets, sewers and curbed, paved streets were built—often with the use of convict labor—and lots surveyed. A city well was drilled to provide fresh potable water for residents and orange trees alike. In 1925, Temple Terrace was incorporated, Gillette was elected mayor and Fowler became deputy mayor.

Elsewhere in Tampa, subdivisions such as Palma Ceia, Beach Park, Sunset Park and Hamner's Forest Hills were also marketed as homes for wealthy and discerning northerners seeking winter homes and perpetual sunshine. Like Temple Terrace, most of these new residential communities featured the game of golf and the idea of exclusivity as their primary selling points. More than two hundred new subdivisions were platted and in the process of being developed in the Tampa area, and more than $3 million in new construction was reported for the first nine months of 1924. Buses, special trolleys and open-top limos made their way through these new areas carrying thousands of potential customers. Special exhibitions by professional boxers, golfers and tennis players drew crowds of thousands, who, once the spectacle of the moment was finished, were encouraged to tour the available housing lots. The publicity machines of Tampa-area developers followed the pattern set in Palm Beach and Miami but did not rise to their level—at least not before the arrival of "Doc" Davis.

Finding the right location in Tampa required some hard detective work, but by early 1924, Davis had settled on several mudflats and small islands he had explored as a young man in Tampa. Located at the mouth of the Hillsborough River, there was not much to recommend the islands, which were frequently submerged, as building sites, but Davis was very familiar with what Carl Fisher had accomplished with dredges on Miami Beach. After some complicated maneuvering, he was able to purchase all of the island property for $350,000. This sum included $200,000 to the City of Tampa, which owned one of the islands, but which the city promised to return to him if he met a four-year deadline to complete the project, erected a bridge to the islands, donated a fifty-five-acre park to the city and surrounded the entire area with a seven-foot sea wall. In addition, D.P. Davis Properties, Inc., his new company created to handle this project, faced a lawsuit by property owners on the banks of Hillsborough Bay facing the proposed new development who opposed his plan to create eighteen hundred feet of new land. Ultimately, an agreement was reached that gave him the right to expand the size of the islands by seven hundred feet. The final hurdle Davis faced was the need to get the U.S. Army Corps of Engineers to approve his plan to dredge soil from the bay to use as fill for his island community. Final approval came on August 7, 1924.

"Doc" Davis, always impatient and confident that he would prevail, blithely went about getting ready for work to begin. He acquired a location on Franklin Street in the heart of the city and, under a strict veil of secrecy, renovated it as a sales office. Opulent furnishings created the impression of an exclusive gentleman's club, and a forty-foot glass-enclosed scale model of his projected development dominated the office. He also began to assemble the advertising and sales staff that would market his creation in the twenty or so offices he opened in other cities. F.W. Montayne, an advertising genius from New England, became the director of advertising; Athos Menaboni, a young Italian artist, was charged with creating the graphics for the ads; and J.P. White, a veteran real estate salesman from Chicago, was hired to head up the sales department. On September 24, the *Tampa Tribune* announced that the noted landscape architect Frank M. Button, who had gained a great deal of fame from his work on George Merrick's Coral Gables, had agreed to oversee the creation of a tropical paradise on the newly reclaimed land. All that remained was to begin the actual reclamation of the as-of-yet unnamed development. The next day, however, the *Tribune* revealed that the new community would be named Davis Islands.

Just three weeks after receiving the final approval of the Corps of Engineers for his dredging operations, Davis signed a contract with the Northern Dredge and Dock Company of Minneapolis to pump nine million yards of fill dirt from the bottom of the bay to create Davis Islands. On October 4, 1924, well before any major improvements to the development were complete, Davis decided to offer three hundred lots—all of them still under water—for sale. Designated the "Hyde Park" section because the area was immediately across the bay from the Hyde Park neighborhood on the mainland, the lots drew a large crowd of buyers, who began to gather outside the sales office on Friday afternoon. After waiting uncomfortably all through the night, they rushed inside as soon as the office opened on

David P. Davis

Davis Islands featured broad avenues, Mediterranean Revival architecture and the obligatory canals for gondolas. Landscape architect Frank M. Button moved from Coral Gables to work for "Doc" Davis in making his reclaimed land a veritable tropical paradise. *Courtesy of the Florida Historical Society.*

Saturday morning, and by noon, all of the lots had been sold. Speculators spent $1,683,582 for nonexistent land, confident that Davis was a man of his word and would deliver as promised. Nine days later, J.P. White's sales force collected another $1 million in land sales.

Twenty-four hours a day, five big dredges dug and sucked soil from the bay, slowly expanding the small islands and mudflats into a large 875-acre development eight feet above the tidal surge in Hillsborough Bay. Quickly, project after project was completed—a French company built the world's largest lighted fountain at the entrance to Davis Islands; three luxury hotels and two apartment buildings rose from the mud to provide visitors with temporary homes; sixty homes were built; and a city hospital was under construction on land donated by Davis. He also leased WDAE, the city's four-year-old radio station, and relocated its studios on the islands, just so every station break would mention its new home—Davis Islands. A country club featured a disappearing roof that opened to the stars, while patrons danced to the music of Isham Jones's nationally known band.

A $100,000 decorative bridge linked the islands with the mainland, replacing the original wooden service bridge. Drawing on every promotional gimmick used by Fisher and Merrick in Miami and innovating some of

The Palace of Florence, an "apartment hotel," provided potential buyers and seasonal visitors spacious and luxurious accommodations when they came to Davis Islands. *Courtesy of the Florida Historical Society.*

his own, Davis offered potential buyers the opportunity to view the entire development by air. A fleet of three hydroplanes regularly circled the project offering rides to prominent local and visiting dignitaries but always ensuring that potential paying customers got a chance to see available lots. He also quickly joined Florida's powerboat association and staged major speed competitions on the "Davis Islands Marine Raceway," a three-stage course that paralleled the shores of the development. Olympic champion swimmer Helen Wainwright was paid $10,000 to swim around the development, while professional golfer Johnny Farrell received a fee of $1,000 to drive a golf ball from the islands to the mainland. Jack Dempsey amazed potential buyers with boxing exhibitions, while tennis aficionados were entertained by the Dixie Cup tennis tournament. Like Fisher and Merrick, Davis operated a system of buses that trucked interested visitors from around the state. A small yacht, the *Pokanoket*, was also used to ferry potential customers from the mainland and to give an "around the shores" tour. Hundreds of visitors took advantage of the free transportation to Davis Islands and the free lunches that the company served—so many, in fact, that Davis was forced to build temporary dining rooms to accommodate them.

David P. Davis

When it came to promotion, D.P. "Doc" Davis proved that he was the equal of any Florida developer. By the end of 1925, he proudly announced that all of the available lots had been sold in a final sale that netted $18,138,000 for his company. An additional $8,250,000 had to be returned to buyers because there were no more lots available. In less than eighteen months, "Doc" Davis took the concept of an island development and turned it into a reality. Although he boasted that he poured $30,000,000 into the creation of his unique development, the sales figures for the eighteen months of 1924 and 1925 tell a different story. Reported sales topped $21,000,000—even with unreported sales, the total probably never exceeded $25,000,000—but Davis, like his contemporaries throughout Florida, tended to count resales as part of the overall total. Despite this minor discrepancy in sales figures, no one could doubt that the Davis Islands project was an unqualified success. Out of barren mudflats and tidal island, a paradise had emerged.

For Davis, however, Tampa was finished, and he looked around for new vistas to conquer. The "Ancient City," St. Augustine, intrigued him, and on October 15, 1925, ten days before he announced the sale of the final lots on Davis Islands, "Doc" let it be known that he was moving his entire operations—dredges, sales force, architects and landscapers—to the fifteen hundred acres he had bought on Anastasia Island. Located across the Matanzas River only a couple thousand feet from the center of St. Augustine, he planned to spend $50 million on the new development, which would be grander than anything he had done before. The *St. Augustine Record* published its largest issue to date, adding Davis's name to the list of great men associated with the city's history. Ponce de León, Pedro de Avilés and Henry Morrison Flagler were united on the front page of the paper as the "movers and shakers" to place St. Augustine in the front ranks of American cities.

Davis Shores, as the development was called, would feature a $200,000 yacht club, a $250,000 country club, an eighteen-hole golf course, a $1.5 million luxury hotel, more than fifty miles of paved streets, one hundred miles of sidewalks and a $200,000 Roman pool and casino. Since the new development would be across the Matanzas River, the old tramway bridge would not be sufficient to handle the volume of traffic during construction or after completion, so a new bridge would have to be built. St. Augustine city leaders decided to construct a new bascule bridge that would cost $1 million. Work on the bridge started in 1925, even before Davis started construction of his development. Guarded by two massive lions made of Carrara marble donated by Dr. Andrew Anderson, a local physician, it was finished in 1927.

With the Davis Islands project sold out by late 1925, "Doc" Davis sought new land for new developments. He settled on Anastasia Island opposite the Matanzas River from St. Augustine. Connected to the city by a small tramway, the new development of Davis Shores was advertised as being bigger and more expensive than Davis Islands. *Courtesy of the Florida Historical Society*.

To make access to the projected Davis Shores development, the City of St. Augustine approved the construction of the $1 million "Bridge of Lions." It was completed after Davis's death and after the end of the land boom. Davis Shores languished unfinished until many years later. It never achieved the glamour that Davis planned. *Courtesy of the Florida Historical Society*.

David P. Davis

On November 10, 1925, Davis opened his initial sales office in St. Augustine and offered the first lots for sale on November 14. By the end of January 1926, he had more than twenty offices operating around the state. Buyers were offered the chance to purchase lots at preconstruction prices, which they were assured would only rise in value. Any potential customer who doubted this statement was referred to the record of what had happened when Davis Islands lots were sold. In less than five hours after the sale began, a total of $11,268,000 had been committed for the first two thousand lots in the development. Another $7,137,000 in commitments was made, and although no more lots were available, Davis announced that he would open a new section of the development for those who had been denied lots in the first sale. Very quickly, a side market developed as real estate brokers sought to buy the lots purchased in the first sale.

Just as he had done in Tampa, Davis set about publicizing Davis Shores. Helen Wainwright, the Olympic swimmer, demonstrated her skills in the water; Will Rogers, the noted social commentator, appeared at the Alcazar Casino under Davis's auspices; international golfers Archie Compston of England and Arnaud Massey of France participated in exhibition matches; and a large-scale model of St. Augustine and Davis Shores, sixty feet long and twenty-two feet wide, created by Fred W. Leist for $50,000, became the city's latest tourist attraction. On January 20, 1926, Davis, true to his word, offered the second section of lots in Davis Shores for sale. Although $18,714,600 in subscriptions was tallied, the reality was that the new section did not sell out. The unsold lots remained on the market until they were removed on March 4.

As 1926 dawned, Davis seemed poised to outdo even his successful development in Tampa. What in the world could go wrong? Almost $30 million in sales had been recorded before the most basic improvements had been made to Davis Shores. The Florida boom continued.

CHAPTER 9

Addison Mizner

Addison Mizner was doing better than ever. Straight-faced critics were comparing his version of Palm Beach with Athens during the Age of Pericles. He was not only society's pet and darling, but also its trendsetter. When he wore his shirttails out to cool his great girth in the warm weather, for instance, the sports shirt was born. Clients pointed with pride to items that Mizner had forgotten to include in their houses—like doors or stairways or bathrooms. It became such a status symbol to own a Mizner slip that people were known to invent them if they didn't exist. He was the stuff of which tall tales were made—a veritable Paul Bunyan of the Palm Beach gossip circuit.
— David Nolan, Fifty Feet in Paradise: The Booming of Florida, *1984*

W hen Addison Cairns Mizner arrived in Palm Beach in 1918, he was looking only for rest and respite from the after-effects of a beating he had received during a robbery. The scion of a prominent California family—his father was the U.S. minister to Guatemala—he had a number of adventures in the Yukon and Europe, all of which added to the Mizner mystique that figured prominently in his later career. After a three-year architectural apprenticeship in the offices of Willis Jefferson Polk in San Francisco and a short period as a partner in the firm, he spent the next decade touring the capitals of Europe. Fascinated by Spanish culture and the gracious style of Spanish architecture, he augmented his income by purchasing religious artifacts and architectural elements, which he shipped back to the United States. Before the outbreak of World War I, he established a practice designing country homes for the wealthy on Long Island. While this provided him with a modest income and a chance to liquidate the various treasures he had purchased in Europe, he felt restricted as an architect. More important for his career in Florida, his sojourn as an architect for the moneyed class in New York provided him with an entrée into the wealthy society in Palm Beach—and the money these elites had and were willing to spend made him the most prominent architect of the Florida boom.

Although a latecomer to development in the Sunshine State—he didn't actually begin to develop his own properties until 1925—his almost total commitment to the use of Mediterranean Revival architecture for the houses he designed for the residents of Palm Beach made him the leading figure in the state. Fisher, Davis, Merrick, Ringling and a host of other smaller developers hired architects to imitate his style for their developments. Although some, like Glenn Curtiss, tried to differentiate the architecture of their developments by referring to it as Pueblo, Mexican Revival or California Mission, the truth was that only a trained architect or a well-informed layperson could detect the subtle distinguishing difference. For the public, the prevailing boom in architecture was simply called Mediterranean Revival, and Addison Mizner became the darling of Palm Beach society and the arbiter of boom architecture.

Like most things in his life, Addison Mizner just meandered into his career as *the* Florida architect. In his book *The Legendary Mizners*, Alva Johnston credits the washed-up boxer Kid McCoy—Norman Selby—with thrusting Addison into the mainstream of Palm Beach design. According to Johnston, Mizner's friend Paris Singer, the heir to the vast sewing machine fortune, was involved in a tempestuous relationship with the famous dancer Isadora Duncan. While Singer was away on a business trip, Duncan discovered McCoy, who was teaching a physical culture class at Gus's Bath, a gymnasium favored by Palm Beachers. McCoy, who had nine legal wives and a plethora of sweethearts, added Isadora to his long list of conquests. By the time Singer returned from his business trip, the boxer had replaced him in Isadora's affections and, to make things even more painful, "had formed the habit of throwing big champagne parties and charging them to Paris Singer's account."

The McCoy episode was not the first time Isadora had played fast and loose with Singer's emotions—there had been numerous other affairs with younger men—and usually the couple would break up for a short time when one of her momentary diversions came to light. Singer, an aficionado of architecture, would console himself with reviewing plans for this or that new building. After a short separation from Isadora, he would usually make amends by surprising her with some costly gift. (After one such separation, he bought her the old Madison Square Garden, which he planned to remodel as a dance studio. She rejected his gift.) This time, however, there was to be no reconciliation, and Singer turned his attention once again to architecture.

Summoning his friend Addison Mizner, Singer outlined his plans for the construction of a large hospital for wounded American officers. Rejecting the prevailing architecture as "institutional," Mizner allowed his imagination to run free and, drawing on his experiences in Latin America, California and Europe, devised a grand building in a style he called Mediterranean Revival. Unable to purchase authentic tiles and other elements of style from Europe because of the German submarines that brought ocean trade to a standstill, he decided to set up his own workshops and manufacture faux replacements. Frustrated at not being able to import ornamental cast stone, he experimented with baking-powdered rock and glue, chilled in an icehouse, to get acceptable replicas. Inexperienced workmen were taught to mold clay tiles for the roof by shaping them on their thighs, while inexperienced roofers were hired to create the impression that the roof had been repaired and added to over hundreds of years. Furnishings, too, were created in new factories and aged by chemicals he purchased from local drugstores. Shellacs, varnishes, sooty candles and lamps, whitewash and a variety of other devices were used to add age and wear and tear to rooms and pieces of furniture. A local blacksmith was taught the intricacies of working with wrought iron to duplicate the railings for balconies. Whatever was needed, Mizner developed a way to produce. When Singer's new building was completed, Mizner bought the small factories and organized them as Mizner Industries, Inc. They became an integral part of his housing business in Palm Beach and later Boca Raton.

Although the war ended and the need for a hospital disappeared before its completion, Paris Singer was delighted with his building and promptly opened it as the exclusive Everglades Club. Although the Everglades Club was an important and beautiful building, Mrs. Edward T. Stotesbury, wife of the noted investment banker E.T. Stotesbury, a partner in the financial enterprises of J.P. Morgan, demanded that Mizner build her a winter palace that would be more beautiful than the Everglades Club. When her thirty-seven-room mansion, El Mirasol, was completed, it was the start of a new career for Mizner. Soon, he built an even larger home for the Joshua S. Cosden family and touched off an ongoing competition among the doyens of the town. Mrs. Stotesbury called him back to enlarge El Mirasol, and Mizner added a forty-car garage, a teahouse, a private zoo and an auditorium. The

Above: Wealthy heir to the famous sewing machine fortune, Paris Singer was the dominant force in the Everglades Club, Palm Beach's most exclusive club. He alone decided who would be allowed to become a member and who would be excluded. *Courtesy of the Florida Historical Society*.

Left: Addison Mizner bought swamp property from "Alligator Joe" Campbell and quickly converted this marginal land into Worth Avenue and Via Mizner, where he maintained living quarters until his death in 1933. *Courtesy of the Florida Historical Society*.

race was on. Mizner became the resident architect for Palm Beach society and embarked on "a career of money and glory."

With the financial backing of Paris Singer, Addison Mizner began to branch out. He purchased an alligator farm—opened in 1891 as a tourist attraction for visitors to Palm Beach—from Joseph "Alligator Joe" Campbell. He quickly converted the low swampy area into a small shopping district, which housed his offices and his showroom of antiques and reproductions. Worth Avenue became home to expensive, seasonally operated stores, while Via Mizner and Via Parigi provided space for small apartments and galleries. Even today, the Worth Avenue district is regarded as one of the most expensive shopping venues in the world.

Although Addison Mizner made a considerable fortune designing homes for the Palm Beach elite, he envied the glamour and public attention garnered by developers like Carl Fisher, George Merrick and D.P. Davis. Always desirous of being the center of attention, he cringed at the thought that these lesser lights—these builders—were capitalizing on his ideas and designs and being hailed as geniuses. No longer satisfied with amusing and abusing patrons in the limited arena of Palm Beach, where his architectural ambitions were always checked by the willingness of the wealthy to pay for new projects, he decided to cash in on the land boom and create his own town. His brother, Wilson, joined him in the scheme.

Wilson Mizner was a charismatic con man whose career carried him from the highest rungs of New York society to the depths of the nation's underworld. Quick witted and immoral, he viewed society—particularly the wealthiest elements—as a playground to carry out his elaborate schemes. Like Addison, his personality and family connections offered the opportunity to move seamlessly into the fabric of high society. His inclination, however, was to mix with the lower rungs, an inclination that made him even more appealing to his wealthy friends. Talented in many ways, Wilson was a playwright, a musician/composer and a raconteur *par excellent*. He served as the model for several Damon Runyan characters, was a favorite party companion of the international set and always provided a quotable quip to fit any situation. Drug addict, shyster, con man, gambler and womanizer—all terms that aptly described him—he merely used these foibles to make himself more interesting. He joined Addison in Palm Beach and oversaw the sales force in his galleries, always operating with the motto, "Take the money; never turn it down!" He fit perfectly into the frenetic environment of the Florida land boom.

Determined to create an entire town built to his specifications, Addison Mizner envisioned a community that would be so magnificent and grand that the great mansions he had designed in Palm Beach would become "servants' quarters" for the residents of his new Boca Raton. Out of low, marshy swampland several miles south of Palm Beach, the Mizner brothers set about creating the world's most exclusive development. The Mizner Development Corporation planned a massive new community, accessible by the world's broadest highway, the El Camino Real. Twenty lanes wide and lavishly landscaped, the El Camino Real was intersected by a canal that featured real Venetian gondolas and real Venetian gondoliers. Although the road ran for barely a half mile, it did what it was intended to do—create the illusion of wealth, luxury, exclusiveness and all Mizner. It was, in Wilson Mizner's words, "a platinum sucker trap."

Drawing on his fame as the architect of Palm Beach and on his connections with the upper class, Addison Mizner quickly assembled a gaggle of imposing personalities to lend their fame to his development. Marie Dressler, Irving Berlin, Elizabeth Arden and T. Coleman du Pont were among the first to pledge their allegiance to Addison and Boca Raton. Some, like du Pont, not only lent their names to the project but also invested heavily. The glitterati wanted very much to be part of the Mizner experience. Harry Reichenbach, the public relations director for the Boca Raton development, marketed the new community with the explicit idea of excluding the middle class through the review of all buyers by a select committee that would ruthlessly weed out the undesirables. Operating on the philosophy that nobody wanted to belong to the middle class, he spent millions of Mizner's dollars fulfilling his mantra of getting "the big snobs, [so] that the little snobs will follow."

When the first lots were offered to the public in 1925, the Mizner Company sold more than $11 million in property. In the first twenty-four weeks, sales exceeded $26 million. David Nolan's description of the hullabaloo surrounding the sale captures the frenzy that attended the event: "Money was literally being thrown at them, as checks had to be gathered up in wastebaskets to await processing." The *Miami News*, which chronicled the Miami boom development, noted that the rich stampeded into Boca Raton much like "the foot race of the original Okies into the Cherokee Strip when it was thrown open to homesteaders in 1893." Although they were late entrants into the race for dollars, Addison and Wilson Mizner—overnight millionaires—moved immediately to the head of the class of promoters.

Awash with cash, Addison Mizner began to implement his plans for Boca Raton. Infrastructure—street paving, water mains, sewage systems—required large expenditures and so, too, did the construction of the one-hundred-room

The dining room at the Boca Club was as plush and opulent as Addison Mizner could make it. Movie stars, members of the ultra elite in America and European royalty wined and dined here. *Courtesy of the Florida Historical Society.*

The magnificent Boca Club was the sugar in the trap to catch the "platinum suckers" who came to Boca Raton to buy an Addison Mizner–designed estate and to be a part of the dazzling social scene. Even today, the Boca Club retains its glamour. *Courtesy of the Florida Historical Society.*

Cloister Hotel, the administration building for the Mizner Development Corporation and the model homes used to sell more lots. Although Wilson Mizner bragged to a friend that he and Addison had squirreled away some $50 to $100 million from the sales of Boca Raton property, this was just another case of his use of hyperbole.

Wilson Mizner left the planning to Addison. He assumed the role of secretary-treasurer for the Mizner Development Corporation, a position he filled with relish. Quickly, he added a Miami office to market Boca Raton, managed to reroute a highway to provide oceanfront for property they owned in Boynton and generally brought disruption and chaos to the operations of the corporation. However, despite his interference, nothing seemed to be able to burst the Boca Raton bubble. The frenetic urge to own a piece of Florida brought millions of people to the Sunshine State, and Boca Raton was among the most desirable properties to own.

It appeared that 1925 would be the year when "the Riviera, Biarritz, Mentone, Nice, Sorrento, the Lido, Egypt—all that charms in each of these finds consummation in Boca Raton." High praise for a development with a Spanish name that loosely translated means "the mouth of the rat."

CHAPTER 10

Lesser Lights and Smaller Fry

Mr. Collier is spending yet other millions in development and draining [the] *Big Cypress Swamp and the Gulf Coast lands adjacent, with the city of Everglade as the center of operations where, until recently, there stood a sign which gave a shock to every true Floridian who saw it: "No Land For Sale Here!"*

In the normal course of Florida events he is due to become the first man to make a billion dollars from land. The Astors, the Rhinelanders and the Goelets made their hundreds of millions in New York City real estate, but the 1,050,000 acres which Mr. Collier bought in Florida for around three million dollars has a potential value of more than a billion dollars when it shall have been drained, cleared and made ready for settlement.

—Frank Parker Stockbridge and John Holliday
Florida in the Making, *1926*

B arron Gift Collier was already a wealthy man when he first visited Useppa Island on Florida's Gulf Coast in 1911. An avid fisherman, he soon bought the island and established a private club there for his friends. Mainland Florida also enthralled him, particularly the wild lands along the southern edge of the Gulf Coast and the Everglades. "Frankly," he once explained, "I was fascinated with Florida and swept off my feet by what I saw and felt. It was a wonder land with a magic climate, set in a frame of golden sunshine." He soon converted his fascination into land purchases, and by 1921, he counted more than one million acres of primeval wilderness as his personal property.

Barron Gift Collier was the single largest landowner in Florida in the 1920s. His 1.5 million acres in southwest Florida were eventually made into a separate county that bore his name. *Courtesy of the Florida Historical Society.*

Barron Collier was born in Memphis, Tennessee, in 1873, the scion of a prestigious southern family that claimed kinship with Virginia Dare, the first white child born to English parents in North America. He reportedly graduated from the elite Oglethorpe College in Atlanta, but a recent article in the *Marco News* (April 20, 2008) marking the eightieth anniversary of the opening of the Tamiami Trail asserts that he dropped out of school at age sixteen to go into business. As a young man, he worked first for the Illinois Central Railway as a sales solicitor. He quit the railroad company when he convinced the Memphis city government to install gasoline-powered streetlights and won the contract to do so. With the profits from this venture, he then purchased a half interest in a small printing company. One of the sidelines of the company was printing small advertising cards, which were displayed in the interiors of horse-drawn streetcars. When electric trolleys and subways became widespread in the major cities and even smaller towns in the United States, Collier organized the Consolidated Street Railway Advertising Company to provide ads for all of the cars. Within a few years, he had established a virtual monopoly on this form of advertising. Even through the minor recessions of the late 1890s and early 1900s, his company and its subsidiaries thrived. By age twenty-six, he was a millionaire many times over.

In 1911, he negotiated a contract with the Chicago Street Railway Company and, in the course of the negotiations, agreed to purchase Useppa Island from the president of the company, John M. Roach. Collier was enchanted and visited Useppa frequently. He also purchased a sizeable orange grove located in the extreme southern end of Lee County from Roach. Near the present-day Everglades City, the raw, undeveloped subtropical landscapes situated on the very edge of the great Everglades "captured Barron Collier's soul," as Charles E. Harner, author of *Florida's*

Promoters: The Men Who Made It Big, wrote. The area certainly motivated him to add more and more land to his Florida holdings.

Walter Fuller, a St. Petersburg real estate dealer and co-owner of the streetcar company in that city, met Collier several years earlier when he and his father had agreed to change their advertising contract from a Tampa-based printing company to Collier's company. When he heard Collier was interested in buying more land in the Sunshine State, Fuller put together a tract of some 400,000 acres of farmland in northern Lee County. When he presented his proposal to Collier, it was rejected. Barron Collier was not looking for developed land at all; what he wanted was raw, wild land that he could "make into a place where people [could] live." He did just that. Between 1921 and 1923, he amassed more than 1.5 million acres of swamplands and cypress forests in southern Lee County.

Collier centered his operations in the small hamlet of Everglade, a quaint fishing and trading village with a population of fewer than twelve families. He immediately brought in dredges to pump fill dirt to raise the town site a few feet above the surrounding swamp. The nearby Allen River was rechristened the Barron River, and a phalanx of surveyors, architects, planners and landscapers began to systematically lay out docks, railroad depots, warehouses, streets and homesites. Within a few months, he poured enough money into the town to change it from a one-horse town to a bustling town with its own power plant and city water supply, a two-room schoolhouse, a medical clinic, a movie theatre and a forty-five-room hotel presided over by Claus Senghaas, a Bavarian chef Collier convinced to immigrate to Florida. The Manhattan Mercantile Corporation, owned by Collier, quickly established a large mercantile store, gas station and petroleum storage facility, which wholesaled gasoline to other stores in the area. To ensure quick and easy communications with his New York–based advertising business, Collier paid for the stringing of telephone and telegraph wires between Everglade (now called Everglades) and Fort Myers. On July 9, 1923, the Bank of Everglades was opened.

The greatest difficulty facing residents of the new town was that of actually getting to it. No roads and very few crude trails existed. James Franklin Jaudon, the Miami tax assessor who owned property in Monroe County, urged the state to build a road from Tampa to Miami (the Tamiami Trail) to link the east and west coasts. Although construction started in 1915, construction on the north–south portion of the highway came to a halt in 1919 when Lee County could not come up with the funds to pay for any more work. The project was revived in 1921 when Jaudon formed the Chevalier Corporation and agreed to fund the completion of the road if the route was changed to go through Monroe County. In 1922, the state also ran out of funds to pay for the east–west portion of the roadway.

With construction halted on the east–west portion of the Tamiami Trail, Barron Collier stepped in. He invited Governor John W. Martin and Fons Hathaway, the chairman of the State Road Board, to a dinner at his home on Useppa Island. The next morning, Governor Martin announced that an agreement had been reached between the men. In exchange for splitting a portion of Lee County off from the whole and creating a new county—90 percent of which was made up of the more than 1 million acres of Collier land—to be called Collier County, and rerouting the road to run through the new county, the developer agreed to fund the final leg (some seventy-six miles) of construction.

With the new roadway under construction, Collier went about completing his plans for making Everglades (now referred to as Everglades City to distinguish it from the Everglades proper) a major port city on Florida's east coast. David Graham Copeland, Collier's engineer, went to work converting the town into a base of operations for the construction crews. An industrial section of the town, Port du Pont, contained barracks and mess halls for workers in the town, sawmills, boatyards and machine shops. While Collier's development of Everglades City proceeded, so, too, did construction on the first "Alligator Alley."

Although much of the surveying for the route had been done earlier, it was necessary to resurvey some parts because the markers had disappeared. A canal, approximately twenty-four feet wide and twelve feet deep, was dynamited out of the Everglades muck. Workers toiled in two ten-hour-a-day shifts, living in temporary shelters and earning only twenty cents a day for their efforts. Turnover was a constant problem and approached 50 percent a month. Workers injured on the job—and accidents were frequent—had to be transported miles across swampy terrain to receive medical attention. Nevertheless, work progressed, often measured in a few feet or a few yards a day. The costs reached astronomical heights, with one estimate of the final cost placed at $25,000 a mile.

The road opened officially on April 26, 1928, two years after the end of the boom. Still, Barron Collier thought it was money well spent. Even though many Florida promoters—Fisher, Davis, Mizner and Merrick—were finished financially by then, Collier was still making an estimated $14,000 a day on his various enterprises, excluding his Florida land developments. By 1933, however, even the once recession-proof advertising business was in the toilet. *Time* magazine reported in its June 22 issue that year:

The Tamiami Trail, a road stretching through southwest Florida across the Everglades to Miami, was the brainchild of James F. Jaudon of Miami. Although construction started on the road in 1915, it was stop-and-go until Collier agreed to finish it in 1923. *Courtesy of the Tampa-Hillsborough County Library System.*

Last week in Tampa, Fla. Barron Gift Collier, famed organizer of car card advertising, virtually declared himself bankrupt. He did not use the exact word. What he said was that he could not pay all his debts immediately and wanted a moratorium. He thus became the first U.S. tycoon to take advantage of the new bankruptcy law which President [Herbert] Hoover signed the day before he left office.

He might have been bankrupt, but he was not broke. Against an estate of some $37 million, he owed $9 million to his various companies and $4.5 million to banks and other creditors. In his Florida portfolio alone were fourteen hotels, three newspapers, a construction company, a mercantile company, the Florida Railroad and Navigation Company, the Inter-County Telephone & Telegraph Company, the Bank of Everglades, an assortment of smaller companies and land—lots and lots of land. Although he had not paid all of his debts by the time of his death in 1939, he remained the largest single landowner in the state. A major participant in the Florida boom, Collier's fate (and good fortune) was to avoid investing millions more in subdivisions. His descendants have profited from his accumulation of Florida lands and continue to do so today.

Glenn Hammond Curtiss became associated with the Miami area in 1912, when he accepted an invitation from local businessman E.G. Sewell to open an aviation school in the city. Curtiss was a well-known figure in American aviation, ranking only behind the Wright brothers. During World War I, his factories produced the famous Curtiss JN04, better known as the "Jenny," which was used to train the majority of American pilots. He was also the innovator of naval aviation, successfully demonstrating how airplanes could take off from the decks of naval ships. In 1919, a Curtiss-designed NC-4 "flying boat" made the first transatlantic crossing. (The city of Miami Springs' official website states that he received the Congressional Medal of Honor [1930] for his work in World War I, but this has been disputed by a number of sources, which found no record of the award.)

In 1916, he moved the school north of the city on land donated by rancher James Bright. He and Bright formed a partnership and soon operated the Curtiss-Bright Ranch together. For five years, the ranch was the largest dairy and poultry farm in the area. In 1921, the two men decided to take advantage of the boom in development and converted parts of their vast holdings into three residential communities: Hialeah, Country Club Estates (later Miami Springs) and Opa-locka.

Glenn H. Curtiss, an aircraft manufacturer and pilot, introduced Pueblo or Mission Revival architecture for his development of Hialeah. Very few untrained persons could tell the difference between this style of architecture and variations of the more plentiful Mediterranean Revival buildings. *Courtesy of the Florida Historical Society.*

Hialeah, billed as the "Gateway to the Everglades," was built on ecologically fragile acres carved from the edge of the Everglades. *Courtesy of the Florida Historical Society.*

Buyers had a variety of choices for the exteriors of their homes. The new city of Hialeah (incorporated in 1925) featured a predominance of Mission-style architecture, which was different from the Mediterranean Revival style that became the hallmark of boom-era developments. As the developers, Curtiss and Bright donated land for schools, churches and other community buildings, but, as one writer put it, Hialeah went "honky-tonk." Advertised as the "Gateway to the Everglades," the city was home to a number of gambling establishments, including a greyhound racetrack, a jockey club and thoroughbred track, a jai alai fronton, an amusement park and numerous nightclubs and juke joints. "Hialeah rye," dispensed across South Florida by countless bootleggers and bartenders, became a favorite with Floridians deprived of more traditional brands of liquor by Prohibition. Although Curtiss and Bright had envisioned Hialeah as "Hometown, USA," the Jazz Age, Prohibition and the land boom moved the town in a different direction.

Curtiss's second development, Country Club Estates, was a more family-oriented community. Broad boulevards, lined with Australian pines, led to a small business district with a circular plaza. A restrictive building code required that all homes built in the development be consistent with the Pueblo style of architecture, meet certain setbacks from the street and have a backyard and prohibited industrial and commercial development. Three golf courses, built around a luxurious clubhouse, provided residents and their guests with a great opportunity to play the game on tournament-quality courses—one of which was designed by Miami golfer Thomas "Tubby" Palmer. Adjacent to the Curtiss aviation school, which would later become Miami International Airport, the development was popular with aficionados of flying. By 1926, some 135 homes, the Pueblo Hotel and the country club were complete. The community was incorporated that year.

Glenn Curtiss's third major development, Opa-locka, featured Persian Revival architecture. The story goes that Curtiss, who was impressed with *One Thousand and One Arabian Nights*, the book he was reading, sent it to his New York architect, Bernhardt E. Muller, to use as the template for the new development. As a result, Muller created "the Baghdad of Dade County," a collection of private and public buildings with domes, spires, minarets and parapets. Street names came directly from the book—Sesame Street, Ali Baba Avenue, Caliph Street, Previz Avenue, Azure Way. Although Curtiss wanted one street named for the heroine of the book, Scheherazade, his marketing staff persuaded him that the name was too difficult to spell and even more difficult to pronounce, so it was shortened to Sherazad Boulevard, which often was confused with another street, Sharar Avenue. Today, many

After Hialeah took on an unsavory character, Glenn Curtiss and partner James Bright developed Country Club Estates (now Miami Springs), which featured three golf courses surrounding a magnificent clubhouse. *Courtesy of the Historical Association of Southern Florida.*

of the homes and public buildings that made up Opa-locka are on the National Registry of Historic Places.

Although the downturn in land sales in 1926 had some impact on Curtiss's development, he determined to keep developing his communities. Unlike other promoters, his fortune—much like that of Barron Collier—came in large part from his manufacturing concerns, particularly his aircraft factories. Even so, by late 1927 and early 1928, it became apparent that the boom was over and Florida real estate would not recover for quite a while.

Joseph Wesley Young, a transplant from California, arrived in South Florida in January 1920 with a vision of creating a "Dream City in Florida," where the arts, particularly movie making, would dominate the life of the town. He was confident that he could buy, build and sell a "city for everyone—from the opulent at the top of the industrial and social ladder to the most humble of working people." He planned a city of broad boulevards—capable of handling twelve cars abreast—bordered by man-made lakes. Three large circles, roughly ten acres each, would provide space for a community park, a government center and a military academy. He created the Hollywood Land and Water Company, which was divided into twenty-six departments, to handle all aspects of developing his new town and to establish strict regulations to govern the kinds of buildings and enterprises to be allowed. Theatres, schools and churches, all part of the master plan for the city, provided a solid moral and intellectual basis for its residents. A thirty-foot-wide concrete promenade paralleled the beach for a mile and a half and provided residents and visitors a chance to stroll the shores of the Atlantic Ocean in comfort. The boardwalk was home to Florida's largest bathing pavilion, which had 824 dressing rooms, eighty showers, a shopping arcade and an Olympic-sized swimming pool. In February 1926, the Hollywood Beach Hotel opened. It was seven stories high and had 500 individual rooms with private baths. Built at a cost of $3 million, it boasted a direct wire connection with the New York Stock Exchange, which kept the northern industrialists and investors, who made it a favorite retreat, in touch with the activities of Wall Street. With its solarium, reputed to be the world's largest, and its fancy ballrooms, the Hollywood Beach Hotel quickly became the social center for local elites. The Hollywood Golf and Country Club, built in the early 1920s, featured a championship golf course and an opulent clubhouse with a large open courtyard that could be covered during inclement weather.

When Joseph Young took stock of his creation in January 1926, he counted more than twenty-four hundred private homes, thirty-six apartment buildings, 252 business buildings, nine hotels either completed or under construction and a permanent population of eighteen thousand residents. His original one-square-mile city had grown to eighteen thousand acres and claimed six and a half miles of oceanfront. Nothing, it appeared, could go wrong!

Weedon Island, now recognized as an important site for prehistoric settlement based on the 1923–24 excavations conducted by Jesse Walter Fewkes of the Smithsonian Institution, was a part of the boom development craze. Eugene Elliot and his partners attempted to make the island the "Riviera of Florida," offering large lots at low prices. The centerpiece of the development was the Narvaez Dance Club, a speakeasy that offered prospective buyers a chance to drink until they were ready to buy. Not a lot of buyers wanted lots on the island because of its remote location and the difficulty getting to it, but Elliot's speakeasy did a booming business. When it mysteriously burned one night (some say because of rivalries between competing bootleggers who wanted to supply hooch to the club), he immediately rebuilt and called his new club the San Remo, which was bigger and grander than the original. A fifty-foot tower attached to the club overlooked the entire island. When the development market collapsed in

The Hollywood Golf and Country Club featured a large open patio where patrons could dance under the stars. The patio was covered by a canvas roof during inclement weather, and the dances could go on. *Courtesy of the Moorhead Collection.*

1926, Elliot lost his island. Although the First National Bank of Tampa, which held title to the island, offered to sell it to the City of St. Petersburg for use as a park, the city could not afford it. In 1929, the bank failed and the island passed to Fred Blair and a group of investors. They immediately began construction of the Grand Central Airport, which opened in 1930. In January 1931, Eastern Air Transport (Eastern Airlines) made the airport its national headquarters and provided the first commercial air service between St. Petersburg and Tampa. From the Grand Central, Eastern also offered air service to major northern cities.

William J. Howey, son of a circuit-riding minister and his wife, was born on January 19, 1876, in Odin, Illinois. At age sixteen, he entered the business world as an insurance salesman, and by 1900, he was a top producer for three companies. At age twenty-four, he went to work developing land and towns for railroads in Oklahoma. In 1903, he opened the Howey Automobile Company in Kansas City, but after making only seven automobiles, he closed the business and went to Perez, Mexico, where he bought a large tract of land. He hoped to develop pineapple plantations with the help of American capitalists, but the Mexican Revolution in 1907 forced him to abandon the venture and move back to the United States and Florida.

Howey was intrigued by the prospects of becoming a citrus grower and perfected his citrus farming skills in the Winter Haven area, where he cultivated citrus groves. In addition, he bought and sold land for new developments. In 1910, he began a second project at Lake Hamilton. He also developed raw land in Dundee and Star Lake. He planned to erect his home on the site where Bok Tower now stands in Polk County, near the famous Mountain Lake Golf Course. However, his focus changed, and in 1914, Howey began buying land in Lake County, which he envisioned as the site for a planned development that he optimistically called the "City Inevitable." Although the entry of the United States into World War I slowed the implementation of his grand design, he pressed forward, and by 1920, he had assembled about sixty thousand raw acres. Bill Howey purchased raw land for $8 to $10 per acre and sold it for $800 to $2,000 per acre after it was cleared and planted with citrus trees.

Howey's intent was to develop the largest horticultural empire in the world. The area and climate were perfect for citrus growth and offered rich, sandy soil with excellent drainage, which was protected from frost because of the one hundred square miles of freshwater lakes that surrounded his holdings. He formed the Howey Company, establishing its headquarters in the city named for him. He announced his plans in a series of lavish advertisements in northern newspapers, and investors flocked to the area. They traveled by barge through a series of freshwater lakes from Jacksonville to Howey's sprawling "tent city," which housed early laborers and settlers. In 1927, he used a fleet of five-forty passenger buses to bring potential customers from his sales offices in Tampa, St. Petersburg, Miami, Palm Beach and other locations. Howey guaranteed investors that their investments, including money advanced for land, planting and grove care, would generate 6 percent interest if the buyer signed a maintenance contract with Howey's company, the Orange Belt Security Company. If the grove did not return the total cost of the original investment, plus interest, by the eleventh year, the Orange Belt Security Company would repurchase the property for a price that equaled the original amount paid out, and only the proceeds from previous citrus crops would be deducted.

The guarantee was irresistible, and the Howey development moved ahead at full speed. A town named after him was incorporated on May 8, 1925. Bill Howey served as mayor from 1925 to 1936. It was difficult to draw a distinct line between the interests of the citizens of the town and those of the Howey Company, since they were often the same. In early 1926, citizens of the new town approved a $300,000 bond issue to fund a citywide water system, thirty miles of paved streets, a fire department and a city hall. In 1925, Howey began construction on his home in the city, and when it officially opened in 1927, he had spent more than $250,000 on its construction and an additional $55,000 on furnishings. The Florida legislature officially changed the name of the original town to Howey-in-the-Hills on May 13, 1927, in order to reflect the beauty of the lakes and hills, which Howey touted as the "Alps of Florida."

Keenly aware that undeveloped land held little interest for most investors, Howey quickly erected the Bougainvillea Hotel, a wooden-frame structure, which became the center of life in the Howey planned community. It burned down in 1917 and was immediately replaced by the Hotel Floridan, a stucco building, adjacent to the Chain-O-Lakes Country Club and golf course. To make sure that the Chain-O-Lakes course was a world-class facility, he secured the services of Chicago golf course designer George O'Neil, who worked with Chicago club professionals/course designers Jack Daray Sr., Joseph A. Roseman and Jack Croke. O'Neil's handiwork proved immensely popular with visitors, and Howey was able to raise the hotel's room rate each year as the demand to play the course grew.

When the Florida boom started to go south in mid-1926, Howey remained confident that the resulting depression would not have much of an impact on his development. He had carefully planned to make the community self-sustaining, and his plan seemed to be working.

From 1915 through 1924, Howey had registered 187 sales, but in 1925 alone, he sold 69 parcels. In 1926, sales of 117 parcels saw more than $5 million poured into the coffers of the Howey Company, which equaled the sales of the previous ten years. Although many Florida promoters had given up the ghost by 1927, it proved to be a banner year for the Howey Company when 127 parcels were sold. Sustaining growth during the "bust" was difficult, and by 1928, land sales had plummeted to only 90 parcels. This was a precipitous decline that continued in 1929 and 1930, when sales of land brought in only $250,000. The number of his employees fell dramatically from the mid-1920s' high of six hundred, and the company payroll dropped from a high of $1.1 million a year to only $101,000 by 1930.

Bill Howey continued to promote Howey-in-the Hills throughout the Depression—or at least until his death in 1938. Between 1931 and 1938, the Howey Company averaged only twenty-eight sales a year, but the company skated along, surviving on the annual maintenance and development fees paid by those who had purchased land. The contracts, challenged by the Securities and Exchange Commission, were eventually declared to be unregistered securities by the United States Supreme Court and illegal—but that was after Howey's death in 1938. That same year, the Howey Company properties were sold to Claude Vaughan "C.V." Griffin. However, through good years and bad, William Howey had persevered, and that fact alone made him an unusual individual among the many "lesser lights" of the Florida boom.

CHAPTER 11

Every Little Nook and Cranny

Florida had discovered golf as an attractive medium of entertaining those who drifted within its borders during the winter months. Now it has embraced and appropriated the game as a prominent industry. The ancient Scotch game surely has had and still holds a definite place in the general scheme of the stupendous developments going on there now...It has come to be a recognized fact that a town in Florida, sending out calls to the visiting legions, that does not have a golf course, is burning good powder in blank cartridges. They simply have to provide their guests with the privilege of reviling a chronic slice, framing the festive alibi, or chortling over the execution of the long putt that hits the back of the cup and plops in.

—"*Golf Courses Dot Florida's Landscape,*"
American Motorist, *October 1925*

There were other developers, although none of them approached the size of Fisher, Merrick, Davis and Mizner in their operations. Around the state, hundreds of smaller developments—usually associated with the game of golf and frequently aimed at clientele from a particular state or region—dotted the countryside. Although golf courses had long been a mainstay for the hundreds of luxury hotels in the Sunshine State, by 1915 a new phenomenon—golf communities—appeared and soon became an important part of the boom frenzy. Northerners, who were limited to playing during the summer months only, eagerly sought venues that gave them the opportunity to enjoy the game year-round. Florida's perpetual sunshine and its balmy winter temperatures made it ideal. So, too, did its location on the East Coast. With the construction of passable roads—such as the Dixie Highway—and strategically located rail lines, Florida was within a two-day ride for the bulk of the American population. Chicago, New York, Boston, Cincinnati and other large cities provided the people, while Florida provided the large open spaces that could accommodate the courses. From the late 1890s until the present, golf course designers have found employment, and today more than fourteen hundred courses give mute testimony to the fact that this phenomenon is continuing. Donald J. Ross, Tom Bendelow and Arthur W. Tillinghast became familiar names to golf enthusiasts who noted their particular styles of designs, while scores of lesser-known designers plied their trade without the fanfare that accompanied these men.

The popularity of golf received a boost when President William Howard Taft (1909–1913) took up the sport as a way to get exercise. Since then, golf has been known as the "Sport of Presidents," and most presidents play the game, although with varying skill levels. With Taft's adoption of the game, the sport became de rigueur for people of importance. Some historians maintain that golf changed Taft from a progressive politician to a conservative one—he vetoed a bill that outlawed child labor—largely because of his contacts with businessmen on the courses. Perhaps. Once the game received the official approval of the president, it was adopted by thousands of politicians, businesspeople, celebrities and the public at large.

Golf was unique in American sports. In its simplest form, the game is democratic in nature, allowing rich and poor to play the same game without any rigid requirements for equipment or dress. It is also democratic because there are no restrictions—except for professional tournament players—on skill levels or experience. Everyone, from the newest duffer to the most grizzled player, can play, even in the same groups. Golf is also nondiscriminatory because there are not prohibitions regarding sex or race. Women, who are among the most ardent enthusiasts of the game, can play alongside men, while African Americans, Hispanics and other races participate equally. Only societal norms—segregation, snobbery, economic status—place limitations on who, when and where golf is played. Today, however, most of these limitations are gone, although some private courses are still restricted to members only. The actual game, however, is indeed the most democratic and welcoming sport ever, but it is also the most demanding.

For promoters during the Florida boom, the one thing about golfers that attracted their attention was their willingness to spend money in pursuit of the sport. Golfers become addicted to the sport, constantly pitting themselves against the courses, demanding more and more difficult challenges and spending more and more money to improve their game with newer equipment, private lessons and membership in exclusive clubs. Few advertisements for Florida developments failed to mention golf as an enticement for investors, and most featured a real or imaginary golfer, in full golfing attire, swinging away on some lushly landscaped course. Chambers of commerce aided in this effort by publicizing the temperatures of the Sunshine State. Miami's chamber informed the public:

> On only six days in twenty-nine years has the temperature gone down to freezing; only once in that period has it reached 96 degrees; the average January temperature is 67 degrees; and the ocean water is above 70 degrees from December to April. There is rarely a day without sunshine, there are seldom fogs, and almost never severe storms [emphasis added].

Tampa assured potential new residents and visitors that

> it is almost ideal, either for the tourist who wishes to escape the faintest reminder that the thermometer has a freezing point, or for the year-round resident who demands that his summer sunshine be tempered by cooling breezes. Ninety-six degrees Fahrenheit is still Tampa's high temperature peak, and it has been reached only once. Even in August the absence of anything approaching the humidity of the northern coast cities or of the burning prairie winds of the Middle West, makes living comfortable in Tampa.

St. Petersburg, which called itself the "Sunshine City," echoed the same story. The *St. Petersburg Evening Independent*, the city's major newspaper, offered its customer free papers on the days it rained and felt comfortable doing so.

Golf enthusiasts took advantage of the climate of the Sunshine State and flocked to it. As early as 1900, dedicated golf communities became popular in Florida, and even during the depths of the bust, golf communities continued to grow. Although Coral Gables, Miami Beach, Boca Raton and Davis Islands received most of the publicity attending the boom, they were multipurpose communities that stressed more than just golf as entertainment. These new developments were located primarily on the west coast and in the center of the state. These were areas that did not receive as much attention from promoters, basically because of the absence of oceanfront venues, but were ideal for the creation of golf courses. St. Petersburg was a favorite area for golfers, and Walter Fuller and other developers offered golf as the major attraction for their developments. In the Panhandle and in southwest Florida, golf dominated advertisements for new communities, although fishing and hunting opportunities were also ballyhooed.

In 1912, Barron Gift Collier discovered Florida when he took possession of Useppa Island. He quickly converted the rudimentary community on the island into a first-class golfing haven enjoyed only by his wealthiest friends and their guests. In the Panhandle, James E. Plew, owner of the Chicago Towel Company, established a vacation home in Valparaiso. In 1923, he established the Valparaiso State Bank to provide him a business base in Florida. In 1924, he constructed the Valparaiso Inn and hired the firm of Langford and Moreau to design and build an eighteen-hole golf course adjacent to the inn. He immediately invited friends from the Chicago area to become members of an exclusive golf club, using the Valparaiso Inn as the clubhouse, known as the Chicago Country Club of Valparaiso. A number of Chicagoans accepted his invitation and decided to spend their winters in the town. Reciprocal memberships in the private clubs of Chicago made it exceedingly popular, and a small community soon developed around the course. The club continued to operate until 1929, when it went bankrupt.

Cleveland real estate magnate H.A. Stahl came to central Florida in 1922 to vacation and to assess the opportunities for investing in land. An avid fan of the Cleveland Indians, who held their spring training in Lakeland, Stahl accepted a 1923 invitation from the local chamber of commerce to come to the town to evaluate the area as a possible site for a new housing development. Stahl was impressed with the region and, in October 1924, purchased 560 acres on the south shore of Lake Hollingsworth for $935,000.

Stahl planned a development similar to his ultra-successful Madison Golf Lakelands and Ridgewood Country Club in Cleveland. Before the end of the year, he sent several members of his staff to oversee the construction of the development, which became known as Cleveland Heights. Streets were laid out, and a sales office was set up at Cleveland Heights Boulevard and Lake Hollingsworth Drive. Photos on the brochure show Model-T Fords in the parking lot, but the palm trees that line the four-lane road today had not been planted.

More than 1,000 lots were platted on both sides of Cleveland Heights Boulevard in late 1924, from Lake Hollingsworth south to Carleton Street and from Florida Avenue on the west to Warrington Avenue on the east. (A framed copy of the plat map hangs on the wall in the Cleveland Heights pro shop.) Stahl named many of the streets, some were paved and about

The Pasadena Golf and Country Club in St. Petersburg went through several owners before it was purchased by attorney Dixie Hollins in 1929. "Sir" Walter Hagen, recognized as the best professional golfer of the period, was the president of the club, and his fame was enough to attract a number of people to the club. *Courtesy of the Moorhead Collection.*

Useppa Island near Boca Grande was a bastion of privacy for Barron Collier's friends who enjoyed playing golf. Even today, Useppa Island remains somewhat restricted and access is limited. *Courtesy of the Tampa-Hillsborough County Library System.*

400 of the 1,080 lots were sold, with two-story Spanish-Mediterranean and Tudor homes going up near the lake. The project also included a four-block business district on Florida Avenue between Allamanda Drive and Kerneywood Street.

"The land is dry, even in the rainy season, and free from the moist, humid conditions that make living so undesirable in some of the low-lying coastal towns," read the company's brochure. Cleveland Heights was a "high grade residential community high up in the Golden Hills of Florida." Salesmen, some of them ballplayers for the Indians, showed the development to prospective homebuyers from Tampa and St. Petersburg, who arrived on a sixty-two-passenger bus.

To provide recreational opportunities for the residents of his new development, Stahl included a golf course and hired Cleveland architect H.P. Whitworth to design the clubhouse. The golf course architectural firm of William S. Flynn and Howard C. Toomey was retained to design a championship eighteen-hole golf course. Stahl also employed one of the nation's foremost landscape architects, Charles E. Swinehart, to oversee the surrounding area. Swinehart, a graduate of the University of Illinois, had taken on similar jobs at Stahl's Madison Golf Lakelands Course and the Ridgewood Country Club in Cleveland. The golf course and the $1 million clubhouse, built on the shores of Lake Hollingsworth, opened with all the flair of an elite Roaring Twenties country club in the spring of 1925. Women in full-length white dresses and men attired in hats, ties and plus fours walked the new course with caddies carrying their hickory-shafted clubs.

Cleveland Heights thrived until 1927, when Stahl's project went under as the bottom fell out of Florida's land boom. Two years later, the stock market plunged, and the Great Depression engulfed the nation. In addition, the hurricanes of 1926 and 1928 made people skeptical about building and living in Florida, and by 1930, Stahl's project was in receivership. The Cleveland Heights Golf Course survived to become one of Florida's top public courses. The clubhouse, which became the Lakeland Yacht and Country Club in the mid-1930s, offered residents lawn bowling, tennis courts and roque (croquet), along with a playground and beach.

In 1923, Carl Dann Sr., a major land developer in central Florida and a talented amateur golfer, became disenchanted with the strict rules against gambling on golf games at the Orlando Country Club and decided that a new, less conservative club was needed. In a single morning, he collected enough $1,000 pledges from friends and business leaders to underwrite a new club. He decided to locate the new course—called the White Stag Golf

Course—in the center of his new 435-lot Golfview Terrace subdivision. With streets with names like Mashie Lane, Niblick Avenue and Brassie Drive, the connection with golf was undeniable. Tom Bendelow designed the course, which was completed and opened for play in 1924. It was an immediate success. Unlike many of the other courses built during the boom, the White Stag—later called Dubsdread—course remained in private hands until it was sold to the City of Orlando in 1978.

In 1915, James F. Taylor opened his Palma Ceia Park as an exclusive community west of Tampa. In order to attract wealthier residents of the city to his new subdivision, he offered a one-hundred-acre plot for the creation of a golf course at very reasonable terms. Members of the Palma Ceia Golf Club agreed to lease the land for $1 a year for ten years and then purchase it for a fixed sum of $150,000. Tom Bendelow, known far and wide as the Johnny Appleseed of golf course designers, was hired to design the course, and it opened for play in 1916. The *Tampa Morning Tribune* ran an advertisement for Palma Ceia on April 18, 1916, which promised:

> *The men and women who are buying Palma Ceia lots (for low prices of $500 to $800) will have cause for congratulations before the summer is over. The opening of the Palma Ceia Golf Course and new country club in August will enhance the value of all the land in the surrounding territory. People of wealth and leisure will build around the course.*

The ad was truthful, and today Palma Ceia remains one of the most exclusive residential areas in Tampa.

To the northeast of Tampa, Temple Terrace beckoned as a mecca for golfing fanatics. In 1914, the Potter Palmer family of Chicago purchased much of this area and used the land as a winter hunting preserve. In 1921, after the death of Beatrice Palmer, the family sold the property to William E. Hamner. Hamner turned around and sold the property to a syndicate led by his brother, Burt Hamner, and his partners, D. Collins Gillette and Vance Helm. This syndicate then formed two corporations. The first, Temple Terraces, Inc., controlled approximately four thousand acres north of Druid Hills Road and dedicated it to the production of the Temple orange, a new variety of orange that the group was anxious to market. The second company, Temple Terraces Estates, planned to build a residential community centered on a fabulous golf resort. The estates included about seven hundred acres bordered by Druid Hills Road on the north, the Hillsborough River on the east, Riverhills Drive on the south and Fifty-sixth Street on the west. Actually, the developers hoped that these two ventures could be combined by selling both homes and grove plots to wealthy retirees. The citrus would provide an annual income, while the couples enjoyed the activities at the country club. By 1925, enough homes had been constructed for the builders to initiate municipal incorporation proceedings, which received the approval of the state legislature in May 1925.

The Temple Terrace Golf and Country Club course was designed and built in 1921 by the renowned architect Tom Bendelow, who had designed the course at Palma Ceia. The club officially opened in 1922, and that is the date carried on the club's logo today. Few of the homes constructed in the Temple Terrace development had kitchens, and residents were expected to take all their meals in the clubhouse restaurant.

Temple Terrace was also home to the Morocco Club, which was completed in 1925. Built in two sections in the manner of Moorish architecture, it had elaborate tiling in the foyer, and the ceiling of the main building was draped with bright-colored silk in thick folds. At the center of the rear wall in the foyer was a mummy case supposedly imported from Egypt. A huge fireplace and a sunken pool occupied prominent spots in the back of the main building, which led to an Olympic-sized swimming pool. A small room on the second floor also served as a gambling casino. All kinds of gambling games could be found with huge sums of money won and lost in a single evening. Evening dress was required of guests. Evening entertainment at the Morocco Club, which featured nightly dining on squab and pheasant, was primarily dancing in the main part of the club. Once billed as the most luxurious nightclub on the west coast of Florida, the Morocco Club catered to high rollers who sipped champagne and filled the dance floor. It was not unusual for the orchestra to receive fifty dollars for playing a single request. Al Jolson and many other famous entertainers of the day performed there.

With the collapse of the Florida boom in the late 1920s, the development of Temple Terrace came to a screeching halt. Although the orange groves planned by the original developers continued to be productive for several decades, much of the property was sold to other parties and converted to other uses. The Florida Bible Institute, now known as Florida College, utilizes parts of the property for classrooms and dormitories. Famed evangelist Billy Graham attended the institute and, so the legend goes, decided on his career path while meditating on the eighteenth green one night in 1939.

To the southeast of Tampa in Manatee County, the Palmetto Golf and Country Club opened on February 23, 1925, at the very height of the Florida boom. Surrounded by the upscale Palmetto Country Club Estates, the course,

Mount Plymouth in Lake County was another golf project that involved Carl Dann Sr. The enormous clubhouse and hotel was designed to have four separate courses extending from it. Because of the bust in Florida real estate sales in 1926–27, only one course was actually constructed. *Courtesy of the Florida Historical Society*.

designed by the firm of Wayne Stiles and John Van Kleek, was described as one of the most difficult in Florida. Despite the widespread support by the local business community, the club could not winter the devastating effects of the bust of the late 1920s. Sold and reopened several times in the next three decades, the property eventually became a drive-in theatre.

In Lake County, a group of business and professional sports figures joined together to create a year-round golf and recreation complex on the site of the five-thousand-acre Pirie cattle ranch. Carl Dann Sr., the developer of the Dubsdread course and the Golfview Terrace subdivision, led the group, which included such noted figures as Connie Mack and Joe Tinker of baseball fame; Lester Beeman, who owned a chewing gum corporation; and Graves Whitmire, who owned two Chicago newspapers. In 1925, architects were commissioned to draw up plans for a 150-room hotel to be at the center of four golf courses, patterned after the greatest courses in the world. Christened Mount Plymouth to avoid confusion with the nearby community of Plymouth in Orange County, Sam Stoltz, a noted Chicago architect, was hired to design unique houses to border the courses. Basing his designs on the Tudor Revival style, he worked to create a fairyland of castles, houses and smaller cottages.

The bust of 1926 and 1927 curtailed the ambitious plans of the club's founders, and three of the projected four courses were never built. The club survived, however, largely due to the unique decision by its incorporators to take a portion of the money received for each lot sale and create an endowment that would pay for the upkeep of the course, clubhouse and other facilities.

One of the earliest golf developments in Florida was the Pasadena Golf Club, the brainchild of Jack Taylor of New York. Realizing that golf was a surefire magnet to draw residents to his subdivision, he hired Wayne Stiles and John Van Kleek to create a tournament-quality course under the supervision of "Sir" Walter Hagen. Hagen, who was recognized as the premier professional golfer of the era, served as resident professional and president of the club for an annual salary of $30,000, an astronomical figure for the period. Originally named the Bear Creek Golf Course, the name was changed to the more exclusive-sounding Pasadena Golf Club to lure members who were more affluent. Although ground was broken for a large clubhouse in 1924, the large salary the club paid to Hagen and the collapse of Florida's economy in 1926 prevented its completion until 1939. Nevertheless, the Pasadena Golf Club attracted a number of wealthy members, primarily because of Hagen's presence; that is, until the full effect of the bust took hold. By 1928, the course had become an unweeded pasture presided over by wild animals that immediately reclaimed it.

In 1929, Dixie Hollins, a wealthy attorney in St. Petersburg, purchased the property and reopened it under the name the Pasadena Yacht and Country Club. Walter Hagen was again hired to head the operation. From 1930 until 1964, the club, along with the Lakewood Golf Club (a municipal course that opened on Thanksgiving Day 1924) and the Sunset Golf Club of the Vinoy Park Hotel as co-hosts, was the scene of the St. Petersburg Open tournament.

In 1925, Aymer Vinoy Laughner, the son of a Pennsylvania oil millionaire, entered the Florida land boom with plans to create a luxury hotel on the banks of Tampa Bay in St. Petersburg. The result was the Vinoy Park Hotel, a Mediterranean Revival structure that was the largest hotel in the city. As part of the hotel property, Laughner affiliated his hotel with the Coffee Pot Golf Course, which was being built by C. Perry Snell, who was developing a high-end residential development on the aptly named Snell Island. There is some doubt as to who designed the original Coffee Pot course, although two of America's top course designers worked in the area. Arthur W. Tillinghast is a likely suspect because he had designed the course for Walter Fuller's Jungle

Club, although there are those who credit Donald J. Ross with its design since he had been responsible for several other courses in the area, including two courses for the Belleview Biltmore Hotel in Belleair/Clearwater. In 1926, William Hickman Diddel was commissioned to reconstruct a new eighteen-hole golf course on the property, which included the Coffee Pot Golf Course. This new course was named Sunset Golf & Country Club.

The Vinoy Hotel and Snell Island were favorites of wealthy families in the Philadelphia area and New York, and the list of prominent individuals who purchased homes on Snell Island reads like a Fortune 500 listing of the day. Babe Ruth, Herbert Hoover, Calvin Coolidge and countless other well-known people visited the hotel and played the course.

In 1932, Snell sold the golf course and clubhouse for $156,000 to D.L. Clark, the candy maker, along with twenty-four building lots. Clark owned a home in Snell's original development, in addition to other properties in St. Petersburg valued at more than $1 million. He continued to operate the course—with the exception of several years during World War II, when the hotel and the course were used as military training facilities—until 1948, when it was sold to the Alsonett Hotel Group.

In nearby Polk County, a group of "snowbirds," led by Pulitzer Prize–winner Edward Bok, purchased the property of William J. Howey and developed a small golfing community known as Mountain Lakes Estates. The course, designed by Seth Raynor, was considered one of the most playable in the Sunshine State. In 1921, Bok commissioned Frederick Law Olmsted Jr. to design a garden "second to none in the country" as the setting for a 205-foot tower containing sixty bells. In Sebring, George Sebring built the Kenilworth Lodge in 1916. The facility featured a twenty-seven-hole golf course and 117 rooms and was easily accessible to northern visitors via the Seaboard Air Line Railroad. Construction began on Harder Hall in Sebring, another golf-oriented tourist hotel, at the height of the Florida boom in 1925. It was completed and opened to the public in 1927, just as the bust was becoming widespread. Like the Kenilworth Lodge, Harder Hall was built because of the nearby railroad stop. Every new hotel and resort touted newly constructed golf courses as its main feature. Even the small beach community of Indialantic, promoted by developer Ernest Kouwen-Hoven, boasted of the Indialantic Hotel and Golf Club and its new course.

At the beginning of the 1920s, Vero was a small town that had barely been in existence for ten years and had been incorporated for only a year. Yet despite its newness, Vero immediately attracted the attention of prominent

The newly built Indialantic Hotel boasted an adjacent golf course. Developer Ernest Kouwen-Hoven created his development to meet a demand from the American middle class for modestly priced homes in the Sunshine State. *Courtesy of the Moorhead Collection.*

northerners looking for an ideal location for winter homes. In 1919, three Cleveland, Ohio residents—Dr. J.P. Sawyer, Edgar Strong and Dr. W.H. Humiston—purchased 160 acres of land on the barrier island directly across the Indian River Lagoon from the small mainland community of Vero. Separated by the Indian River from the mainland, the property, first known as Southern Dunes, would become one of the most exclusive enclaves in the Sunshine State, restricted to families that met the social and financial standards of the original founders. Quickly, the founders began to build large homes—most without kitchens—in the development. Residents took their meals at the clubhouse, which was completed in 1919. Arthur McKee, a prominent local promoter a few years later, was the first guest to stay in the clubhouse and built the first home in the development in 1919. Six additional homes were soon finished. Among the first homes constructed that year was "Orchid Oaks," built by New York attorney Winchester Fitch, who suggested that the community's name be changed to the Riomar Country Club, a combination of the Spanish words for river and sea.

Alex McWilliams was hired to supervise the construction of a clubhouse and a nine-hole golf course, which was designed by Herbert Strong. The new clubhouse, built in 1929, had room for seventy-eight guests and served as a residential facility for the many visitors who came to the development.

The Riomar Club got its start in the early 1920s and maintained a nine-hole golf course until 1963. It was a very exclusive development in Vero Beach, which "was a community of professionals in the early days. First people from Cleveland came, then those from New York and then Chicago. Mostly they were people who knew each other and heard about Riomar through word-of-mouth." *Courtesy of the Moorhead Collection.*

The clubhouse was the center of activity for the development, and each evening residents of the community would gather there for cocktails, despite the fact that Prohibition was the law of the land. Eventually, ownership of the Riomar Club passed into the control of Paul K. Semon and the Riomar Corporation, who sold it in 1965 to St. Edwards School.

In 1920, the private nine-hole golf course was completed, and residents could add this sport to swimming in the Atlantic Ocean, tennis and fishing. The course had the distinction of being the only course between Daytona and Palm Beach. On an inspection tour of the newly constructed Intracoastal Canal in 1921, President-elect Warren G. Harding, who was also from Ohio, was persuaded to play a round of golf on the new course. Harding's visit to Riomar added to the prestige of the development, and the demand for property there accelerated, but this demand was not met. The original nine-hole course was expanded to eighteen holes in 1963, and membership in the Riomar Country Club was opened to individuals who were not property owners in the original Riomar development.

Vero Beach was very much an active and attractive participant in the Florida land boom that swept across the United States in the 1920s, but when the boom collapsed in 1926–27, the Royal Palm development and the Vero Beach Golf and Country Club fell on hard times. Without a constant stream of eager new purchasers to buy homes, memberships in the club dwindled. When the Great Depression followed the bust a mere two years later, the great influx of new buyers came to a screeching halt.

Whitfield Estates in Sarasota, which opened in 1926, featured a championship course designed by Donald J. Ross, who also designed the course for Pinecrest in Avon Park. Pinecrest also opened in 1926. Ross was a prolific designer in the 1920s, and his name was enough to draw golfers from around the world. The San Jose Golf Club in Jacksonville, which opened in 1925, featured his design. So, too, did the Timuquana Country Club, which was chartered in 1923, as well as the Jacksonville Municipal Golf Course, later known as Brentwood and which no longer exists. All of these courses had one thing in common—they were lures to bring tourists and homebuyers to the Sunshine State. Municipalities in Florida, eager to gain their shares of the tourist trade and just as eager to demonstrate their desirability as places for permanent residents, climbed on board the golf bandwagon. Sunshine and beaches were simply not enough.

CHAPTER 12

Shut Your Damn Mouth!

One of the biggest problems with which Florida is at present concerned is that of "truth in advertising," and truth in the news which comes or purports to come from Florida. While it cannot be said of our people that they have been backward in proclaiming the advantages of their State to the rest of the world, neither can it justly be said that the advertising, news and magazine publicity emanating officially or quasi-officially from Florida the State, or Florida communities, has ever been fanciful or untruthful.

The position we take is that the truth about Florida is good enough. We are certain of the future of our State. In 1924 more than $450,000,000 of northern capital was put into permanent Florida holdings. Most of this capital was brought by individuals and corporations familiar with the State. There need be no concern on their account...We are concerned, however, for the small investor. It is his savings which the unscrupulous operator endeavors to obtain.

—Herman A. Dann, President, Florida Chamber of Commerce, 1925

Just when everything seemed to be going well for Florida developers, the bottom fell out. After two years of incessant trading in land titles, the upper limits of reason had been reached, and there was no place higher to go. Speculators who counted on being able to resell properties repeatedly saw the frenetic and constantly churning land market suddenly turn calm. In northern newspapers, the first protests against the boom came when bankers, apprehensive about the loss of deposits to Florida banks, questioned the safety of investments in Florida developments and urged their customers to keep their funds in their banks. The Florida boom, they pronounced publicly, was over. When a New York sportswriter speculated in his column that the boom was dead, a Florida newspaper replied vehemently in an editorial: "Shut Your Damn Mouth!"

Out-of-staters, long deluged by millions of fanciful words by the world's greatest advertising experts, began to take notice of the negative reports and slowed their march to the Sunshine State. Their apprehensions seemed justified by several different occurrences that grabbed the headlines during the final six months of 1925. Overwhelmed by the large numbers of passengers coming to Florida and the large number of freight cars filled with building materials waiting to be unloaded in Miami and Jacksonville, the Florida East Coast Railroad imposed a moratorium on further shipments. Two thousand cars were parked in the railroad yard in Miami because neither warehouse space nor manual laborers was available to unload them and store the supplies. In Jacksonville's Baldwin yard, an additional seven thousand or so rail cars clogged the rails. Only passengers, fuel, livestock and perishables were allowed on the rails. New construction came to a halt, and hundreds of projects already underway—large hotels, apartment buildings and individual homes—were left unfinished in the hot Florida sunshine. Prospective buyers, tourists and workers were unable to find enough housing, which exacerbated the desperate situation.

Alternative systems of transporting needed supplies were explored. The FEC considered a plan to double track its existing lines, but that was expensive and would take months to complete. Competing railroads, such as the Seaboard Airline, announced that they would build new tracks south, but once again, time was a critical factor, and engineering new routes could not be done overnight.

The developing system of highways in the Sunshine State was not a viable alternative. Most were little more than gravel-coated tracks that could not sustain heavy traffic by trucks—if enough trucks had been available—so that option of relieving the shortages of materials was out of the question.

With Florida's long coastline and multiple port cities, the use of ships to carry the critical supplies to keep the boom going was seen as the answer to the dilemma. However, steamship lines discovered that they, too, suffered from the same problems experienced by the railroad. Too few warehouses and too few workers meant that ships were queued in the ports waiting and waiting. In Miami, city employees and convicts were pressed into service to relieve the shortages, but as docks piled high with supplies, the shipping lines were forced to institute their own embargo on noncritical supplies. Building materials and furniture were embargoed. T.H. Weigall, a new arrival in Miami in 1925, described the scene:

> *As usual, every berth was filled. Outside in the harbor, a number of ships lay at anchor waiting to unload…During the last six months of 1925 there was an average of thirty ships constantly in Miami harbour, either unloading or waiting to unload; and this despite the fact that the great passenger lines from New York did not come into the harbour at all, but transshipped their passengers into tenders in the open ocean.*

Despite the fact that larger ships took up most of the space in the harbor, enterprising contractors sought to relieve the bottleneck by putting antiquated schooners into operation to bring in supplies, docking them at small areas of the docks that were between the steamships. A few small towns, unable to get supplies through Miami or Jacksonville, sought to take advantage of the newly completed Intracoastal Canal to bring in construction materials. In Eau Gallie in Brevard County, city leaders spent $90,000 of taxpayers' money to purchase a small steamboat to haul supplies for its developers. Within a year, the *City of Eau Gallie* was sold to a private buyer for $25,000 because by then the boom was dead and there was no need for supplies.

The scarcity of housing for workers added to the problems for Miami. Few rooms were available at reasonable prices, and with no place to live, workers avoided the port. When a group of entrepreneurs attempted to relieve the situation somewhat by towing a decommissioned ship, the *Prins Valdemar*, into port to use as a floating hotel, it went aground and capsized in the channel. For twenty-five days, the port was completely blocked to any traffic. What was happening in Miami and Jacksonville had an impact on smaller developments around the state. In Tampa, labor shortages and the scarcity of warehouse space added to the woes of developers on the Gulf Coast. The slowdown that affected development on the east coast was soon felt on the west coast.

By the beginning of 1925, promoters understood that the boom had taken a new direction; it was now time for the dreams created by publicity agents and promoters to move from concept to reality. Buyers who had purchased empty lots now expected to see houses, amenities and town centers built. Although the sale and resale of lots continued at a high pitch, promoters and state officials stepped in to halt the frenzied activities of unregulated speculators. Binder boys were outlawed from operating from their briefcases or hip pockets; real estate sales were restricted to realty company offices; local real estate regulatory boards were established to monitor the activities of agents; and agents were required to have a state license. In addition, a law was passed that limited the legal lifetime of a binder; it was reduced to ten days, and no additional trades, noted by stickers attached to the document, would be honored. Even the binding percentage required to obtain control of a piece of property was increased.

The embargo on building materials presented real problems. Unable to get supplies, building contractors were forced to halt construction in residential areas, and many went bankrupt. As the number of contractors decreased, chambers of commerce placed large ads in magazines and newspapers in an effort to recruit new ones to take their place. Contractors who remained in business were forced to use inferior materials, and substantial Mediterranean houses, which had first been constructed with hollow terra cotta tiles, were now being built with wooden studs wrapped in chicken wire and plastered over. The illusion of solidity was still there, but the quality of construction was gone. The impact of the change to flimsier construction methods would be graphically demonstrated in September 1926, when South Florida was hit by a devastating hurricane.

By the end of 1925 and the beginning of 1926, promoters and investors had other problems. The Sixteenth Amendment to the U.S. Constitution had established an income tax system that imposed significant levies on capital gains, particularly short-term capital gains on property and stocks held for short periods. The fantastic profits made by investors and speculators during the height of the boom—ballyhooed again and again in the advertisements of developers—attracted the attention of federal tax agents, and they descended en masse on the Sunshine State to collect the government's share. Although most real estate contracts called for payments to be made in three or four increments spread over several years, the Internal Revenue Service demanded its share of the selling prices upfront and in full. Individuals who made thousands of dollars in paper profits now faced demands for payment of thousands of dollars in cash to the federal government in a single payment. Developers who accepted sales contracts worth millions were liable for taxes on the face amount of the contracts, not on the actual amount collected. Exacerbating the situation were the "uncountable cases" of buyers, who

> *being so carried away by the atmosphere* [of the boom] *that they had, on the spur of the moment, bought huge tracts of land, public buildings, or anything else that happened to be offer*[ed]*, without there being the remotest*

possibility of their being able to pay so much as the initial deposit when the time arrived.

Despite Florida's attempt to alleviate a part of the tax burden by the passage of an amendment to the state constitution outlawing forever the imposition of an income tax, the federal government had no such limitation and demanded its money.

Changes in the money supply also presented difficulties for the large and small developers of the Sunshine State. The negative publicity in the northern news media created a reluctance on the part of large insurance companies and investors to shift funds to Florida. Although state leaders ballyhooed the strength of Florida banks, both national and state, and cited the growth of bank deposits from $187 million in 1920 to $263 million in 1924 to $375 million in 1925, the reality was that insider loans and lax reporting made most of them little more than shells. In some cases, loans to officers and staff exceeded the assets of the banks. State and federal regulators, intimidated by political pressure or motivated by urges to enter private banking businesses, noted these irregularities in various banks but failed to take actions to correct them. The assets of many of them were predominantly in the form of landholdings or loans on developments, which depended on the continuing boom to retain their value. The Standard Statistics Company of New York warned in 1925 that

> *by far the larger portion of the purchases of lots and acreage throughout Florida represents speculation pure and simple, the prospective buyers planning neither to plant crops nor to build homes. Until the land reaches the hands of the "ultimate consumer"—the man who will utilize it for the purpose for which it is best adapted*—these values will have no stability and will provide merely the basis for speculation [emphasis added].

Yet, as quickly as deposits poured into banks, they went out for real estate loans. It was an untenable situation for the long haul.

Newly elected governor John W. Martin, a Jacksonville lawyer who worked for several banks, attended a public relations event in New York City in October 1925, along with some of the most prominent Florida promoters, such as Barron Collier, George E. Merrick and N.B.T. Roney and the president of the Florida State Chamber of Commerce, Herman Dann. The purpose of the meeting was to convince major newspaper and magazine publishers that the negative news about the Florida boom was deliberately being printed to cripple the state. The very idea that they could print that the boom was over was ludicrous indeed, since there had never been a boom in the first place. The argument advanced by the governor and the Florida attendees was that the economic activity that had produced the term was merely the market adjusting to the reality of the value of Florida land. What did not exist could not fail. This simple statement became the mantra for the promoters and officials of Florida. Frank P. Stockbridge and John H. Perry summed up the argument succinctly in the 1925 book *Florida in the Making* when they wrote, "The activity in Florida land, viewed as a whole, is not a 'boom' in the sense that prices generally have been inflated beyond actual present values. On the contrary, Florida property has been sold too cheaply!"

The Investment Bankers of America held its annual meeting in St. Petersburg in December 1925, just a few weeks after the governor's New York event. The fabled "Sunshine City" in the Sunshine State was in the midst of a cold, rainy and gloomy season that dampened spirits and hardened hearts. Unable to enjoy the golf courses in the area or to swim and fish in the Gulf, the more than one thousand bankers, who controlled the bulk of the nation's financial institutions, spent their time asking hard—and largely unanswered—questions about investments in Florida real estate that promised 6 percent per year. The failure of the state's bankers, governmental officials and promoters to provide persuasive answers resulted in a vote of "no confidence" in future investments. Not even the argument that supply and demand would determine the ultimate value of any commodity such as land gained any traction. Although Florida had more than twenty-two million tillable acres as yet untouched by development—far in excess of demand—few of the bankers bought the argument that the abundance of undeveloped land meant that the prices being paid in Miami, Boca Raton, Coral Gables, Miami Beach and elsewhere were too cheap. Overall, the conference produced only added skepticism from the bankers and was little more than a black eye for the state.

Although some promoters, such as D.P. "Doc" Davis, established companies that used their own money to fund home construction, they were few and far between. Carl Fisher, who was independently wealthy and had little dependence on loans from banks, catered to a wealthy clientele who could fund their own construction. George Merrick borrowed heavily from banks and insurance companies but put the money to work making his Coral Gables project a reality. Barron Collier, another multimillionaire, invested millions of his own money in southwest Florida, using his personal fortune to underwrite his developments. As promoters went, these men were reasonably honest.

Addison Mizner and his brother Wilson, on the other hand, had little in the way of personal fortunes to undertake their Boca Raton development. With only his reputation and social contacts to go on, Addison nevertheless plunged into the business in a large way. High society's darling, he was able to attract investors from some of the most storied names in the world of finance in the United States. Wilson Mizner, an admitted con man and a convicted felon, had a similar reputation among the glitterati of the American theatre and movie industries, the sports community and even the underworld. Together they made an appealing team, intent on claiming their share of the Florida dream. When they announced their newest development, Boca Raton, they watched as the rich, near rich and wannabes spent millions in opening day sales to claim the finest lots in the development. The biggest problem they had was in deciding whether their promotions were honest efforts to build an exclusive community for the wealthy or whether it was an elaborate con designed to separate them from their money. While Addison might have harbored dreams of creating a town that would be a living testament to his architectural skills, Wilson had no such illusions. Boca Raton, he said, was "a platinum sucker trap." That summed up the Mizner brothers' attitude toward Boca Raton.

The Mizner brothers started their Boca Raton development in mid-1925, late in the game. Using the factories he had purchased from Paris Singer as a base for his new company, the Mizner Development Corporation, Addison Mizner called on his society friends to invest in the company. Soon, he could count a long list of America's wealthiest as stockholders in his company, headed by T. Coleman du Pont, former president of the giant chemical company of the same name and a sometime U.S. senator from Delaware. He became the figurehead chairman for the Boca Raton project, although he soon fell out with the Mizners over the extravagant claims they made about Boca Raton, particularly when one of the Mizner publicity agents, Harry Reichenbach, ran advertisements about a multimillion-dollar development program that didn't exist. The ads contained a single line that urged investors to "attach this advertisement to your contract for deed. It becomes a part thereof," which du Pont felt made him and the other directors of the Mizner Development Corporation potentially liable for any losses they might incur. It was more than he was willing to risk. He was getting out of the Boca Raton business.

"General T. Coleman du Pont was the man who killed the Florida boom," wrote Alva Johnston in 1953. While he was an important public figure in promoting Mizner development, du Pont's decision alone was not enough to stop the madness. He participated in Governor John Martin's New York protest against negative publicity in mid-1925, so when he announced, "This thing [Boca Raton] is sure to fail with these people in charge," his words sparked exits by other prominent investors. Wall Streeters Jesse Livermore and Matthew Brush, taking their cues from du Pont, also departed. Others followed.

More than $21 million in Boca Raton real estate contracts flowed into the coffers of the Mizner Development Corporation, but Addison Mizner spent lavishly, and by early 1926, the company was insolvent. Part of the problem was that buyers paid only a portion of the purchase price initially, and the remainder was to be paid in later installments. Construction of company buildings, infrastructure improvements and personal spending by the Mizner brothers had depleted the company's treasury. Despite the defection of his most prominent backers, Addison Mizner plunged ahead.

Mizner found a temporary solution to his money woes when he and several partners acquired control of the Palm Beach National Bank, with deposits of approximately $300 million. By the end of the first quarter of 1926, deposits had grown to almost $450 million as investors put their cash into the bank instead of real estate. Raymond B. Vickers's amazingly detailed book *Panic in Paradise* unlocks the intricacies of how "Mizner and his partners followed the money into the bank's vault." The bank became a subsidiary of the Mizner Development Corporation and financed the final months of the Boca boom. Through a complicated series of insider transactions, interlocking directorates, interest-free loans to federal and state politicians, unsecured loans to principals and regulators and a host of other unethical and often illegal business practices, Mizner and his associates drained every bit of liquidity from the bank.

The Mizner Development Corporation also had access to deposits in several state banks. By offering sweetheart deals to locally prominent bankers, Mizner gained control of these banks as well. Soon, every bank in Palm Beach and West Palm Beach was involved in sustaining the bankrupt Boca Raton development. The depositors in Palm Beach County were not the only unwilling and ignorant supporters of Addison Mizner's grand schemes. Through the chain of two hundred interlocking banks created by James R. Anthony and Wesley D. Manley, depositors in Georgia, Florida, New York and New Jersey were at risk. The same unscrupulous—many outright fraudulent—practices allowed the Mizner group to use these financial resources as their personal piggy banks.

So much money in Palm Beach banks was tied up in Mizner's Boca Raton project that even the slightest wobble in the fortunes of his company could dramatically affect the stability of these financial institutions. When Guy C. Reed, a stockholder in the Mizner Development Corporation, filed a suit against it for engaging in fraudulent advertising while insolvent, the result was a run on the Commercial Bank and Trust Company of West Palm Beach. This bank, presided over by Thomas Cook, another stockholder in Mizner's company, was unable to meet the demands of depositors seeking to withdraw their money because it had been looted by insiders. On June 28, 1926, the bank closed its doors permanently, and depositors lost all their money. The failure of the Commercial Bank triggered a statewide banking crisis.

On June 29, 1926, with nothing much left in the till, the Palm Beach National Bank closed its doors. It was just the beginning. A panic had set in, and depositors in every bank in Florida felt compelled to see to the safety of their money. The Manley-Anthony chain banks, which had appeared to be so solid and had underwritten millions of real estate loans, were next to collapse. Within two weeks, eighty-three banks in Georgia, the chain's home base, failed. Because of the interstate connections between banks, the failures in Georgia created a new round of failures in Florida.

In October 1926, Edward C. Romfh, mayor of Miami and president of the First National Bank in that city, penned a commentary on Miami banks that appeared in the *American Motorist* magazine. "There have been some failures of small banks through the State," he wrote, "due for the most part to their connection with a chain banking system. In a great many instances these failures are being replaced by new organizations of sound capital structure, which is in line with the general trend toward stabilization." By the end of 1926, over 150 banks in both states had locked their doors.

Although some of the major developers believed that 1926 would see new heights in real estate purchases, some did not. D.P. "Doc" Davis was a believer. In January 1926, he was going full steam ahead in the creation of his latest project, Davis Shores in St. Augustine. By March, the project was dead in the water. He anticipated receiving more than $4 million in payments for property sold at his Tampa Davis Islands development, but he collected a measly $30,000. It looked as if Davis Shores would never get built. Desperate for cash, Davis sold the controlling interest in Davis Islands to a Boston syndicate in August 1926 for $2.5 million and its agreement to complete the project. Not much money, but he needed every penny.

Carl Fisher left Miami during the summer of 1925, right at the very height of the land boom, to create the "Miami Beach of the North" on ten thousand acres he had purchased on Montauk Point on Long Island. Wary of the baseless rise in real estate prices and skeptical about the future profits to be made, he consolidated his holdings on Miami Beach, took some property off the market altogether, upped the required down payments for lots and shortened the time to pay off the remainder. He took his fortune (now estimated at $50 million) and headed north, although he retained considerable properties—including hotels—on Miami Beach.

George Merrick was a believer. Despite the cracks in the real estate market that had first appeared with the transportation embargo, he plunged ahead promoting a new development that would turn a chain of islands in Biscayne Bay into the South Sea Isles of Coral Gables. With a projected price tag of $250 million, his new scheme far outstripped the $150 million in sales he had gotten for his Coral Gables property. He was certainly optimistic.

Outside Miami and Boca Raton, other developers proceeded to build their dreams. Although the frenetic boom atmosphere that had smothered South Florida in 1924 and 1925 was slowly fading, the central and southwestern regions still hummed with activity. In part, this was because many of the developments in these areas focused more on attracting golfers instead of speculators. By hyping the advantages of having a home where the game could be played year-round, developers appealed to a smaller, although more financially stable, clientele.

However, even the most optimistic developers were about to be challenged beyond belief—and the most apprehensive naysayers would have their most negative pronouncements confirmed.

Chapter 13

It Is Over!

Florida hurricanes are much like Chicago bandit outbreaks. Their occasional occurrences do limited damage over a highly restricted area and occasion no concern to the great mass of residents who go about their business as usual without giving them a thought. They are news, when they do happen, just as a snow-storm that breaks up the Rose Bowl festival in Southern California is news. News is the record of the unusual event, and the more unusual the greater its news value. Yet there are some folk who…are afraid to go to Florida because they once read news of a hurricane.

— *Frank Parker Stockbridge and John Holliday Perry,*
So This Is Florida, *1938*

Faced with failing banks, declining real estate sales, inclement weather during the 1925–26 winter season, negative publicity, the failure of many buyers to honor their sales contracts and the Palm Beach/Boca Raton Mizner scandals, it was difficult to believe that things could get worse in Florida. Difficult to believe, but on September 17, 1926, this difficulty was resolved when a devastating hurricane hit Miami and South Florida in the early morning hours. Miami residents had been warned, although not forcefully, as early as September 15 that three tropical storms were churning in the Atlantic. When one of the storms passing between Nassau and the Florida coast brought heavy rains to the area on the sixteenth, the *Miami Daily News* warned that the city might suffer further damages from the storms. At noon on the seventeenth, the

Miami Weather Bureau posted warnings of an imminent major storm, but it was not until eleven o'clock that evening that actual hurricane warnings were posted. By that time, most of Miami's residents were in bed, so the warnings were for naught.

There had been no major hurricanes in the state since 1910, and few residents, new or native, were prepared for the storm that hit. When the howling winds struck in the early morning hours, the winds reached 125 miles per hour and produced a fifteen-foot storm surge in Miami and the barrier islands. The city of Miami experienced severe flooding as water swept from Biscayne Bay into the town. The majority of the coastal inhabitants of the area, unfamiliar with the dangers of a hurricane and ignorant of the impending strike, remained in their homes.

The storm left behind a wide path of death and destruction. Many new residents, inexperienced in the way that hurricanes operate, braved the first onslaught of the storm inside shelters, but as the calm eye of the storm came overhead, they rushed out to see what damage had been done. Richard Gray, who headed the Miami Weather Bureau, reported, "The lull lasted 35 minutes, and during that time the streets of the city became crowded with people. As a result, many lives were lost during the second phase of the storm." The backside of the storm then struck, and many were caught in the maelstrom that followed. In Miami and Miami Beach, the damage was estimated at $100 million, or roughly $2 billion in 2005 dollars. Scarcely a single building escaped damage.

Miami and Miami Beach were not the only cities to feel the force of this Category 4 storm. Slowly, the hurricane made its way across the Florida peninsula and into the Gulf. In the center of the state, the winds generated a significant storm surge on Lake Okeechobee, which broke a portion of the muck dikes that surrounded it and flooded the small town of Moore Haven, another boom-era town developed by James A. Moore. After clearing the state on the eighteenth, the hurricane entered the Gulf of Mexico, pivoted and headed for Mobile, Alabama. When it struck land again, it devastated large areas of the Florida Panhandle.

Almost four hundred hundred persons lost their lives in the storm and another sixty-five hundred were injured. Some fifty thousand families had some damage to their homes, and those houses built since the embargo on building materials suffered the most. Virtually none of the municipalities struck had enacted building codes to ensure that houses could withstand potential hurricane damage. Fewer still had enough code enforcement personnel to ensure that minimum standards were met. Total property

It Is Over!

The devastating Category 4 storm that struck Miami in September 1926 left a path of destruction across South Florida. Here, workmen repair telegraph and telephone lines to reconnect the city with the rest of the United States. *Courtesy of the Historical Association of Southern Florida.*

damage (in 2005 dollars) was more than $157 billion, which makes it the most destructive hurricane on record in the United States.

The hurricane caught everyone by surprise, and they all reacted differently. Mayor Edward C. Romfh of Miami denied press reports that the damage was excessive and informed the American Red Cross and other relief agencies that no assistance was needed from them. In Tampa, Peter O. Knight, the most prominent man in the city, joined him and warned that calling for outside assistance would do more damage to the image of Florida and the boom than any relief funds could do good. Hotel operators, worried about the upcoming winter season, also downplayed the damage done; however, there was no denying the pictures of destruction that flooded the nation's media outlets. What had been a trickle of criticism of the Florida boom became a torrent, and northern bankers and civic leaders took every opportunity to point out the dangers of living in the Sunshine State.

For Florida promoters, explaining the storm became the job of public relations agents who immediately dubbed it a "once in a lifetime storm,"

The Roney Plaza Hotel, newly opened, suffered great damage to its adjacent casino and swimming pool. Florida promoters labeled it a "once in a lifetime storm," but another Category 4 storm hit just two years later. *Courtesy of the Florida Historical Society.*

unlikely to be repeated for another century. In an interesting twist of logic, some promoters and civic leaders pronounced the storm a good thing to have happened, since it cleared undesirable elements from the scene. Although water and wind damaged thousands of homes, the basic infrastructure—roads, sidewalks, sewage systems, water systems and power lines—remained largely intact. Even the man-made islands of Miami Beach, Davis Islands and Fort Lauderdale survived with little damage, resisting the forces of nature that tried to sweep them back into the ocean. The hurricane, so the argument ran, had simply removed structures that were poorly designed or built with inferior materials. In response to the widespread destruction of buildings, John J. Farrey was appointed the chief building inspector for Miami Beach, and he initiated the first building code in the United States. The standards he created were adopted by more than five thousand cities in the United States. Even today, building codes in Florida are governed by the "Miami Standard." Florida was back on track and ready to resume its building boom.

The same month that his op-ed piece defending Florida banks and the state's failing banking system appeared in the *American Motorist* magazine, Edward C. Romfh, mayor of Miami, joined Edward E. "Doc" Dammers, mayor of Coral Gables, along with developer George E. Merrick and the presidents of the two cities' chambers of commerce, in announcing, "Business

It Is Over!

<u>as</u> <u>usual</u> in <u>Florida</u>…The sun is shining. Our people are cheerful and are putting their shoulders to the work of reconstruction. I predict that Miami will make a world record in coming back." Certainly, Miami's hoteliers were keeping their fingers crossed.

George Merrick and Dammers, who was the head salesman for Coral Gables in addition to serving as mayor, assured prospective buyers that the development was "lightly hit by the West Indian hurricane…The total damage to homes, hotels, public buildings and shrubbery did not exceed $1,500,000, which is only one per cent of the money actually invested in buildings in Coral Gables." Everything was under control, they went on to write, and "the organized work of reconditioning started within two hours after the storm subsided."

Ernest N. Smith, editor of the *American Motorist*, added his support:

> *Miami is more than a city. It is an American institution. And it may be expected that the people who have built it into a thriving metropolis in a comparatively few years and have made it one of the outstanding resort cities of a continent will not only stage a speedy come-back, but will reconstruct on a firmer foundation than ever.*

Of course, the fact that businesses in Miami had purchased an entire section of the magazine, which was "in the hands of the printer prior to the disastrous hurricane," certainly had no impact on Smith's willingness to endorse the idea that the boom would continue stronger than before.

Although some promoters continued to build and a few (mainly golf) communities opened, the "everybody wins with Florida land" syndrome was no longer controlling the state's economy. Still, it was difficult to abandon the idea overnight. George E. Merrick was sure that his new South Sea Islands of Coral Gables development would reignite the nation's fervor for Florida, but he was wrong. A year later, he was broke and reduced to operating a fish camp in the keys until another hurricane demolished it in 1935. He eventually went back into real estate as a broker and managed to do quite well. In 1940, he was appointed postmaster of Miami. He died in 1942.

Within a month of the September hurricane, D.P. "Doc" Davis, with tremendous resources committed to Davis Shores, abandoned the state entirely. Davis Shores, his projected exclusive development in St. Augustine, was left to languish in the unforgiving Florida sun. By mid-1927, it was described as "treeless and devoid of top soil; and the white sand tends to drift badly in a high wind…a serious drawback to the comfort and beauty

Mrs. A.O. Weeks of Dania shows the fickle nature of hurricane winds in this 1926 photograph. The winds removed one entire wall of her bathroom but left the fixtures intact. *Courtesy of the Historical Association of Southern Florida.*

of the property for home purposes." It went into receivership. Davis, however, was spared the ignominy of seeing Davis Shores and his Davis Islands development deteriorate. On October 9, he set sail for Europe on the *Majestic* with his paramour and youngest son. What happened next is still unresolved.

Davis disappeared. On October 13, A.Y. Milam, the vice-president of Davis Properties, received a wireless message from the ship that informed him that "Doc" was lost at sea. What really happened, no one knows. The ship's captain ruled his disappearance a suicide, claiming that he had taken his own life by climbing through a porthole in his cabin and jumping into the ocean. Friends insisted that Davis, who delighted in playing jokes on his friends, had been entertaining them by balancing his small body in the porthole when a wave hit the ship and tossed him out. That was the explanation Sumter E. Lowry's insurance company bought, and it paid out a $300,000 settlement. Nevertheless, rumors persisted that his disappearance could be laid elsewhere. One rumor circulated that Davis, who carried a large amount of cash on his person, was robbed and his body thrown overboard. Another insisted that "Doc" had salted away millions and sought to protect them from lawsuits that were bound to follow his failures to complete Davis Islands and Davis Shores. He had arranged, the rumormongers stated with conviction, for a motorboat to meet him mid-ocean and take him to Latin America, where he lived out the rest of his life in well-heeled anonymity. Take your pick; the fact was, Davis was gone.

In Boca Raton, Addison Mizner was drowning in a sea of lawsuits, debts and charges of fraud. He refused to show remorse. The Mizner Development Corporation was purchased by the Dawes brothers—Charles, Rufus and Henry—but Addison continued to try to make money off the Boca project. Through a number of complicated intercompany transactions, he transferred assets and made loans in the name of Mizner Industries, Inc., and Addison Mizner, Inc., two companies he retained. Even though the world was aware of his unscrupulous prior dealings, he was able to borrow hundreds of thousands of dollars in loans, all of which he defaulted on. With his sagging fortunes bolstered by additional loans from wealthy friends, he held court in the Via Mizner Building on Worth Avenue in Palm Beach until his death in 1933.

Wilson Mizner, whose once mega-million-dollar fortune disappeared in the bust, made his way to Hollywood, California, where he went to work for Warner Brothers as a screenwriter and a partner in the Brown Derby restaurant. Like his brother Addison, he held court nightly, surrounded by a coterie of celebrities, underworld cronies and hangers-on. He, too, died in 1933, completely unrepentant for whatever misdeeds he had committed during the Boca Raton craze.

Glenn Curtiss, whose fortune included much more than paper promises on Florida land, continued to be a believer in the return of the halcyon days of the mid-1920s. He held on to much of the acreage he and Bright had bought earlier and, up until his death in 1930, continued to make plans for more development. Joseph Young, whose Hollywood-by-the-Sea development was touted as the "Enduring City," suffered tremendous losses from the hurricane. Over one thousand homes were destroyed completely and another two thousand suffered extensive damage. Young, who had been in New York seeking additional financial support, was wiped out. No additional financing was to be had from anyone, and the Hollywood development went into receivership.

Carl Fisher suffered along with the other Florida promoters. By 1927, his once mighty fortune had been halved as tourism numbers decreased significantly for his hotels in Miami Beach; many of the supposedly "gold-clad" investors in his properties defaulted on the commitments; and the Montauk Point project demanded more and more of his resources. Topping the list of drains on his fortune were the hundreds of thousands of dollars he had to spend to repair the damage inflicted by the hurricane. Still solvent, he was optimistic that stability would return to the marketplace and that he would be able to regain much of the money he had lost. All he needed were a few good years.

No one could deny that the real estate boom in Florida was teetering on its last legs. Every attempt to resuscitate it seemed to be checkmated by another natural disaster. The destruction wrought by the 1926 hurricane was followed by one of the coldest winters on record. Even when warm weather returned in 1927, the economy remained depressed, and real estate sales did not even reach the level of sales for 1924, the first strong year of the boom. To add insult to injury, on September 16, 1928, a Category 5 hurricane swept through South Florida. Although the eye of the storm came ashore near Palm Beach, and although the total estimate of physical damages was significantly lower than the total for the 1926 hurricane ($1 billion in 2008 dollars), the toll of human lives was much higher. The dikes surrounding Lake Okeechobee burst and flooded the low-lying farm areas for fifty square miles, drowning thousands of African American migrant farm workers. Although the exact number of deaths is still unknown, official estimates go as high as forty-one hundred. Bodies, according to one survivor, "were stacked like cordwood" to be buried in mass graves or large funeral pyres. Few caskets were available, and those few were used for white victims. Even today, the controversy surrounding the recovery and burial of bodies continues in South Florida, and African Americans point out that the one mass grave site with a memorial contains only white bodies. Such was the system of segregation that ruled in the South.

The hurricane of 1926 seriously weakened the Florida economy, but the hurricane of 1928 drove a stake into its heart. The land boom was absolutely over. With the end of the boom, the rest of the state's economy went into a deep depression. Although it took a few more months for tourism to decline substantially, decline it did. On September 28, 1929, another, though less destructive, hurricane struck the Miami area and produced additional damage. Three people were killed. It was the coup de grâce.

Not even the collapse of the stock market a month later in October 1929 had much of an impact on Florida, simply because there was little left to have an impact on. It was over.

CHAPTER 14

Of Bottom Feeders and Small Bumps

During the years 1924–25, the state had a "super" boom that brought with it the making of fortunes and also the loss of many. Fundamentally, the state at that time was not in a stage of development sufficient to reap the advantage of such spectacular activities. The overwhelming demand caused by the influx of new residents, speculators, workers and tourists gathered momentum to the point where one development bringing money and workers appeared to justify other developments, and finally this tide of growth necessarily reversed itself when the projects became complete. But the intervening eleven years have done an enormous amount toward healing the wounds of that period.

The definite percentage of growth in population each year due to natural causes, together with the steadily increasing influx of tourists and those in retirement making Florida their home, have caused most of the buildings that were left vacant at the recession of the 1924–25 "super" boom now to be occupied.

— Harry H. Kellim, Coming! Another Florida BOOM!, *pamphlet, 1936*

Try as they might, Florida boosters found it tough going to persuade the American public that everything was going to be all right in the Sunshine State. Frank P. Stockbridge and John H. Perry tried to do so in their book *Florida in the Making*, published in 1926. Was the boom over, they asked? Well, no, they answered, because there had never been a boom to begin with. "The activity in Florida land, viewed as a whole, is not a 'boom' in the sense that prices generally have been inflated beyond actual present values. On the contrary, most Florida property has been sold too cheaply." This became the mantra of those who still believed that recovery to 1925 levels was possible, but it was almost like talking to themselves. Never again, at least not for several decades, would real estate prices approach anything like the 220 percent increase in home values that marked the years 1924 and 1925. Neither would there be a return to the days when millions of dollars could be made on an investment of land purchased for a few thousand—at least, not until many years later. In the words of one St. Petersburg developer, "We have simply run out of suckers!"

Granted, there was some improvement in the numbers of tourists who visited the Sunshine State in 1927 and 1928 (and even 1929), but many of these were holdover reservations from previous years. Others were individuals who had investments in the stock market, and 1928 and the first half of 1929 were good years for them—and, of course, everybody knew that bubble would never burst. Somehow, so the Florida optimists reasoned, the continued growth in the value of stocks and bonds augured well for a return of boom conditions. Even Stockbridge and Perry saw a connection between the activities of traders on Wall Street and the land boom in the Sunshine State. "One might as well ask whether the Stock Exchange rests upon a sound and stable base," they argued, questioning the underlying values of Florida real estate. Their question was answered in October 1929.

There were other ventures in Florida that reignited hopes that the bust would soon be a thing of the past. One was a miniboom in oil exploration. In 1927, J.L. McCord, a wildcatter from Oklahoma, drilled a deep well at Monticello and brought up soil saturated with crude oil, but further drilling produced nothing. That same year, John Ringling, Owen Burns, J.H. Lord and the Palmer family group in Sarasota invested $100,000 in a company headed by Kenneth Hauer of Miami to undertake exploration operations on land Ringling owned in southwest Florida. The city was ablaze with "oil fever," and a public meeting was held to attract more investors. Hauer, aware of the attitude of many Floridians about any new speculative adventures, warned the Sarasotans to be wary of unsound schemes but then promised, "If oil is really found…there will be glory enough and money enough for all, it means another awakening for Florida. It means untold prosperity." B.F. Alley, the site geologist, promised that huge deposits would be found in just three months and assured the crowd, "The real estate boom was a mere shower compared to the cloudburst of money that is coming to this section with the oil boom—and that boom is coming just as sure as we are seated here." The State of Florida encouraged the speculation by offering a

$50,000 prize for the first producing oil well in the state. (It was claimed by the Humble Oil Company in September 1943.) Even though Ringling and his sister-in-law, Edith, leased more than sixty-five thousand acres to Hauer's company, the oil boom went nowhere. All it did was provide a small and temporary bump in the state's flat economic landscape.

Movies, which had originated with the Kalem Studios in Jacksonville, seemed to offer some hope for the flagging Florida economy. Metro Pictures, which would later become MGM, opened its first studio in the city in 1915. In 1920, Richard E. Norman purchased the bankrupt Eagle Film Studio in Arlington, outside Jacksonville, renamed the company Norman Studios and began producing westerns, action films and romances aimed at a strictly African American audience. The impact on the overall Florida economy created by the Norman Studios operations was minimal and limited primarily to the black community. Still, it was something positive.

Other studios in Florida moved to California, where the terrain offered a greater diversity than did the flat Florida plains and where the drier climate meant more days per year for outside shoots. Joseph Wesley Young, the developer of Hollywood-by-the-Sea, thought that Florida would make an excellent rival to California, and he tried to bring moviemaking back to the Sunshine State. Although Young went bankrupt before he could realize his dream, the idea remained attractive.

In 1933, Sun Haven Studios opened on Weedon Island in Tampa Bay. T.C. Parker, a man with movie experience, convinced the island's owner, Fred Blair, to back his dream of a studio facility on the island. Using the old San Remo Club as a sound studio, Parker and Blair planned to make twenty-four movies initially. They quickly found the club building unsuitable and built a larger soundstage, the Kennedy Studio Center. The first of what would eventually be three movies made on the island started filming on May 22, 1933. *Chloe, Love is Calling You* was a small success and led to the filming of the second movie, *Playthings of Desire*, which opened in St. Petersburg in September. The industry was impressed, and so were the people of Florida. Buster Keaton visited the studio and was so impressed that he considered bringing his own production company to the island. He wanted to wait just a little while to make sure the studio would succeed. It was a wise decision.

The third and final movie filmed on Weedon Island by Parker and Blair was *Hired Wives*. Just as the movie was ready to be released, federal tax agents descended on the studio and closed it down for failure to pay taxes. They confiscated the prints of all three movies, the equipment and the new soundstage. Although the studio was leased to Walter C. Martin for two years, he could never get the operation going again. The movie industry was just another tiny—and temporary—bump for Florida's failed economy.

The economic destruction wrought by the collapse of the Florida boom and the physical damage caused by the hurricanes of 1926, 1928 and 1929 attracted bottom feeders who came to the Sunshine State to take advantage of the distress. In Boca Raton, the Dawes brothers, including Vice President Charles Dawes, swept in to glean the few dollars left from the Mizner debacle, and in their wake, they left even more damage. The Central Equities Corporation, led by Rufus C. Dawes, promised to bring the Boca project to completion in return for a controlling interest in the Mizner Development Corporation. Through a series of questionable transfers, the Dawes brothers wound up with most of the remaining assets and none of the liabilities. Although they had promised initially to invest $1.5 million in the company, they advanced only 10 percent of the agreed-upon amount. When the smoke cleared, the Dawes brothers wound up with all of the assets of Mizner's company, including sixty-seven lots, almost eighty-eight acres of land and $10.5 million in outstanding purchase contracts. Once the company had been stripped of virtually everything of value, the company went into bankruptcy. This left about 175 creditors with nothing but $4.1 million in unsecured claims against the corporation. Although it took three years for a settlement to be reached, these creditors received only .001 percent of their claims.

The real estate holdings, which were held by the Dawes brothers, were sold to Clarence Geist, who had been an original stockholder in the Mizner Development Corporation and a former partner of Vice President Dawes, for a paltry $76,350. Rufus and Henry Dawes then became stockholders in his new syndicate. Bottom feeders!

Carl Fisher, who had predicted the end of the boom in Miami and had taken his cash to start a new development, Montauk Point on Long Island, still owned considerable hotel property in Miami Beach in 1926. Through careful oversight of his managers, he was able to keep them profitable through 1928, but with the collapse of the stock market in October 1929, revenues began falling. The Montauk Point project continued to drain his resources. So, too, did a costly divorce and a new marriage.

Seeking to duplicate his Miami Beach success on Long Island, Fisher discovered that his biggest competition came from the long-established watering holes of the northern rich, and no amount of slick advertising could overcome his competitors' advantage. In addition, the Florida bust had made most investors leery of putting money in developmental projects, and he was forced to underwrite the cost of building his project almost entirely. The failure of many banks in the aftermath of the stock market failure dried up the last remaining money sources. Nevertheless, he held on, determined to grab victory from the jaws of defeat. His problems were exacerbated by the failures of his peripheral investments and by his increasing reliance on alcohol to ease the pains of a soulless marriage and declining income.

In Miami Beach, notorious criminals, including Alphonse "Scarface Al" Capone, purchased homes in the most exclusive parts of the town beginning in 1929. By 1932, Miami Beach's reputation was that of a mob-controlled town where gambling and crime ran rampant. Certainly, the Miami Beach of the 1930s was vastly different from Fisher's dream of an exclusive enclave for the newly rich. By 1934, his Montauk Point development had gone belly up after he defaulted on loans and taxes. The only remaining asset he had was the Bayshore Company, which operated the hotels he had built on Miami Beach, but control of that corporation passed into other hands, and he was reduced to living on a fixed salary. What first started as a $50,000 a year salary was gradually cut to a mere $10,000. One by one, he sold off his possessions, including his home—which became the Beach and Tennis Club, a gambling establishment operated by two crime figures.

Gradually, the effects of his increasingly large booze habit, physical illness and depression took their toll. Fisher died in 1939, a financial failure. Interestingly, however, he was named one of the Fifty Most Influential People in the history of the Sunshine State in a 1998 survey by the *Lakeland Ledger*.

George E. Merrick suffered much the same fate as Carl Fisher, although his life did not end as tragically. Without a large personal fortune, he built Coral Gables on a pyramid of credit and loans. With the devastating hurricane of 1926, followed by unusually cold winters and a second hurricane in 1928, the foundations of this pyramid began to crumble, eventually causing a complete collapse. Within months, he and his wife were reduced to operating a small fishing camp on Matecumbe Key, where, in 1935, another hurricane destroyed the camp.

Gone was Merrick's ability to shape the destiny of the city he had created, but his ideas lived on after he lost control. The University of Miami, to which he had pledged $5 million and to which he actually gave $1 million, was a reality that lived on. However, in the face of such adversity, George Merrick pressed on. In 1934, he and his wife formed George E. Merrick, Inc., a successful real estate firm. He became chairman of the Dade County Zoning Commission, served as a director of the Fairchild Tropical Garden and, in 1940, became postmaster of Miami. In 1939, along with Gaines

R. Wilson, he devised a strategy for creating the Historical Association of Southern Florida, an entity that is alive and flourishing today.

George E. Merrick died in May 1942. He left a legacy of a man who dreamed big and failed big but always had the best interests of the larger Miami community at heart.

David Paul Davis, unlike Merrick, did not survive the first bust in 1926. Unable to meet the financial demands of completing his Davis Islands project and terribly in debt with his Davis Shores development in St. Augustine, he vanished in the mid-Atlantic—a victim of depression or robbery or the perpetrator of the greatest disappearing act since Harry Houdini. Like Merrick, he did leave an enduring legacy with Davis Islands, but his Davis Shores project "died aborning."

Harry Eagle, a small developer in St. Petersburg whose Eagle Crest development opened in late 1925, lost it to creditors. He returned to New York, where he soon cornered the silk market but lost everything because rayon, a synthetic and cheaper fabric, became available and replaced silk in the textile market. Unable to handle this second failure, he committed suicide in 1928. D. Collins Gillette, one of the major players in the development of Temple Terrace, also lost his fortune when the boom collapsed. Once a partner of Barron Collier and August Heckscher, he died virtually penniless in the early 1930s. It was a story repeated time and time again. Think big, borrow big, build big and lose everything.

Alfred I. du Pont, among the wealthiest persons in the United States, moved to Florida to take advantage of the depressed economic conditions that followed the 1926 bust. With a personal fortune of $34 million, he was perceived as the savior of the Florida economy when he first arrived in Jacksonville and took up residence. Along with all that money, du Pont brought his brother-in-law, Edward Ball, who would soon earn the nickname "the Machiavelli of Florida politics" and whose alliance with the notorious political "Pork Chop Gang" from the Panhandle made him the most dominant force in the state. Ball was du Pont's factotum, the "doer" who effectively and ruthlessly carried out Alfred's wishes.

Du Pont was interested in investing in land and banks, not in the developments of South Florida or the flimsy chain banks that participated in the thievery that brought about the bust. And he was not interested in building great communities, but rather in acquiring vast areas of undeveloped land and creating a financial institution that was as solid as any other in the world. He quietly started to accumulate land in the most inaccessible part of the Panhandle, which had escaped the frenzied developers of the boom era—hundreds of thousands of acres, enough to make even Barron Collier envious. Ed Ball was there to make his desires a reality.

He acquired the Florida National Bank in Jacksonville and used it as the linchpin in banking operations that spread to Orlando, Daytona, Lakeland, Miami and St. Petersburg. His conservative philosophy in banking ensured that the Florida National Bank and its subsidiaries remained liquid and actually grew during the bust and the Great Depression. His financial resources protected them during runs, and, as David Nolan wrote, to keep them that way,

> *Ball scurried across the state by plane and car to deliver cash where it was needed, guarding it himself with a shotgun (in whose use he had become proficient as a boy, serving as night watchman of the family oyster beds).*

The FNB invested heavily in defaulted municipal bonds because they could be had for very low prices and because du Pont was certain they would eventually be redeemed. It was an act of faith on du Pont's part, but it was also helpful to the state's distressed communities, although some critics accused him of being predatory by doing so.

There was also a progressive political side to Alfred I. du Pont. Even before his arrival in the Sunshine State, he had engaged in creating civic programs. In Delaware, he had financed a pension plan for elderly citizens out of his own pocket and continued to fund it until the state, embarrassed by his generosity and its failure to enact a similar program, took it over. In Jacksonville, he anticipated the New Deal by creating a public works program that paid unemployed workers to clean the streets and do the upkeep on city parks. Just before his death, he and Ed Ball worked out a plan to start a paper mill on his land in the Panhandle and to surround it with a model town that included schools, a hospital and other basic community institutions. Although he died in 1935 before the plan became a reality, he left $58 million to ensure that loyal Ed Ball would carry it into fruition. While he might have gotten richer from his Florida dealings, Edward I. du Pont was no bottom feeder. The jury is still out on Ed Ball.

Some optimists pointed to the continued development of smaller golf-oriented developments in the state as proof that the boom was not over. However, their claims of a building "bump" were not based on a realistic reading of the overall economy. Much of the building that took place in 1927 and 1928 came as a result of "money already in the pipeline" or commitments made before the collapse. Many of these developments were forced to scale back on the original elaborate plans and lasted only a few years. Some developments were left unfinished as funding dried up, and they were reclaimed eventually by nature.

No one, not even the most enthusiastic supporter of the boom, could escape the realization that the bubble had burst, the good times were over and the likelihood of them coming back any time soon was nil. The Stock Market Crash of 1929 ushered the entire United States economy into the Great Depression, but for Floridians, it was not a new experience.

CHAPTER 15

A New War—A New Boom?

> Hope springs eternal in the human breast;
> Man never Is, but always To be Blest.
> The soul, uneasy, and confin'd from home,
> Rest and expatiates in a life to come.
> —*Alexander Pope*, An Essay on Man, *1734*

The bust came so fast in late 1926 and 1927 that there seemed to be nothing that could be done to stop it, but after enjoying such unlimited prosperity, few people doubted that the collapse was anything more than a temporary glitch. After all, Florida was Florida, the state where dreams came true. Florida boosters promised that the bust was temporary, merely a readjustment in the marketplace where the inflated speculative prices would automatically be brought into line with the true values of Florida land. The same boosters promised a new boom, one that would focus on industrial development and the exploitation of Florida's unlimited natural resources—agriculture, minerals and oil. All that was needed was time, but time was the one commodity that was not for sale.

When the stock market imploded in October 1929, any hope for a recovery in Florida died. The same problems—speculation, unsecured lending, wild and reckless buying and selling—that plagued the Florida boom played out on the national scene. Millionaires found themselves penniless overnight, workers discovered that their jobs were gone as factories closed and did not reopen, public employees—teachers and professional employees—were reduced to accepting scrip as payment for wages or having no wages at all and thousands lined up for free food at soup kitchens. There was little assistance forthcoming from any governmental agency.

Cities that had issued bonds to fund new projects defaulted on payments. Some cities that had expanded their boundaries to include new developments repealed their annexations because there was simply no money to pay for city services. Ad valorem tax assessments provided no relief because most of the levies went unpaid. The State of Florida offered little assistance. In a rush to aid new investments in the state during the height of the boom, an amendment prohibiting the collection of income taxes forever had been added to the state's constitution, and this single act, still in force, greatly hampered the state's efforts to aid in any organized recovery. Only the seven cents a gallon tax on gasoline provided any significant income, and by law, that income had to be shared with counties. Many African Americans, who had provided much of the agricultural labor and the manual labor on development projects, were unable to find any work at all and began to leave the state in large numbers, headed north. In a few months' time, the Depression ended their hopes of finding work there as well.

Florida's population, however, continued to grow during the decade of the 1930s by slightly more than 400,000 new residents. The number of cities with populations in excess of 2,500 people went from fifty-eight in 1930 to seventy in 1940, an increase of almost 300,000 urban dwellers. The number of persons residing in the countryside also increased, although by only 50,000. Overall, the 1930 census marked the first time the state's urban population (51.7 percent) outnumbered the rural population (48.3 percent), a trend that continues today.

Herbert Hoover, fresh from a highly effective job heading the relief effort for the Mississippi River flood of 1927, was elected president. Based on his experience, he was expected to solve immediately the economic woes of the nation. His task, difficult enough with the collapse of the Florida boom and the resulting failures of southern banks, soon became even more onerous when the stock market also collapsed. Hamstrung by its conservative economic philosophy, the Hoover administration provided little in the way of aid for individuals or governments. At first, Hoover called on Americans to embrace volunteerism as a way to pull themselves out of what was now called the Depression. While his call might have sounded good, the reality was that no coherent plan for such action emerged from Washington. Finally, Congress attempted to impose some order on the chaotic banking scene when it created the Reconstruction Finance Corporation in 1932 and set aside $2 billion for assistance to state and local governments, banks, farm mortgage associations and other businesses. Unfortunately, he appointed former vice president Charles Dawes to head the agency and soon (as could have been predicted based on Dawes's Florida history) the agency was awash with scandals involving insider deals and political considerations. It failed miserably but continued in existence and was revamped into a more effective agency under Franklin Delano Roosevelt.

Hoover, who had been praised as the "great humanitarian" for his relief work, further damaged his reputation when General Douglas MacArthur used the army to attack and destroy the camp of veterans seeking a quick payout of a promised bonus. Although he had not given the order to do so and MacArthur acted on his own, Herbert Hoover was condemned for the action. He went from "great humanitarian" to the "most hated man in America" overnight. Although he ran for reelection in 1932, he lost the election by a lopsided electoral vote of 472 to 59.

However, hope springs eternal in the human breast, and with Roosevelt's election, all Americans—particularly Floridians—looked forward to improved conditions. In reality, Roosevelt's New Deal program continued many of the policies toward business of the Hoover administration, but his creation of make-work programs provided the bulk of the population with at least some small modicum of income. The "alphabet" agencies—CCC, WPA, PWA, NYA—provided work for thousands of workers and students. The creation of the Social Security Administration meant that additional thousands of older workers would also be withdrawn from the pool of workers seeking employment. Roosevelt's "banking holiday," which shut down banks with the promise that they would not be reopened unless they were stable, and the creation of the Federal Deposit Insurance Corporation by the Glass-Steagall Act of 1933 went a long way to assure Americans that it was safe to put their money in banks.

Did the New Deal work? This is a large question that has been vigorously debated by historians and economists for decades. Certainly, it appeared to work for Florida. In 1937, Frank P. Stockbridge and John H. Perry, who published *Florida in the Making* in 1926, wrote a new book, *So This Is Florida*, which detailed a new real estate boom:

> *The pressure of the growing population upon housing facilities had become so great by the middle of 1937 that Florida was beginning to*

experience another real estate boom, of proportions almost comparable to that which reached its climax in the winter of 1924–25 and collapsed the following year.

But they assured their readers, "The new real estate boom is, however, of a different order...The present real estate boom in Florida is based upon an actual pressing demand for the people who are coming to Florida faster than Florida is prepared to house them." It was a far cry from the earlier boom that had "degenerated into frantic, speculative gambling in land without regard to values, as speculative as the stock-trading on margin which ended with the market crash of 1929."

Of course, any pronouncement by Stockbridge and Perry was suspect since these were the men who, in 1926, had pronounced the boom as being as solid as the stock market itself. Interestingly, *Florida in the Making* had included an appendix with a detailed analysis of the economic situation in Florida in 1926, while *So This Is Florida* had a single appendix entitled "A Guide to Florida Fishing."

It took World War II to lift Florida out of the doldrums. Between 1940 and 1950, Florida's population grew by 46.1 percent, of which 66.1 percent came from people moving into the state. Much of this was due to the location of more than sixty training bases in the Sunshine State, particularly bases for training air corps and naval pilots. Some three million soldiers and sailors received training at Florida installations during the years 1941–45. In addition, the U.S. government located a number of POW camps in the state, while Tampa and Jacksonville were heavily involved in producing ships for the navy and merchant marine. So many new jobs were created by war industries and military bases that the resident population was unable to fill them. Labor recruiters went as far north as West Virginia and as far west as Arkansas to find needed workers. This demand for workers ended the Depression in the state, and the accompanying housing shortage for service personnel and workers depleted the surplus of housing that had existed since 1927. When the war ended in 1945, some of the larger bases remained open and continued to provide jobs. What the war did for Florida, it did for most of the remainder of the United States.

One of the benefits Florida gained from having so many military personnel stationed in the state was a considerable increase in the number of tourists who came to visit them. In 1940, about 2.3 million tourists visited the state, and with the outbreak of war, that number continued to grow each year until it reached about 3 million by 1945 and 4.2 million by 1950. By 1960, the total number of annual visitors exceeded 11 million. Some of these tourists had been formerly stationed in the Sunshine State, liked what they saw and returned with their families for a visit. Still more contributed to the rapid growth in the permanent population of the state when they returned to make Florida their home.

Just as had happened at the end of World War I, Florida was primed for a new boom.

Epilogue

What has been will be again, what has been done will be done again; there is nothing new under the sun.
It was here already, long ago; it was here before our time.
There is no remembrance of men of old, and even those who are yet to come will not be remembered by those who follow.
—Ecclesiastes 1:11, Bible (New International Version)

Just as technological developments—airplanes, the internal combustion engine, the Good Roads Movement—had altered the Florida landscape after World War I, so, too, did the technological developments of World War II alter the Sunshine State. Chief among these was the widespread use of **d**ichloro**d**iphenyl**t**richloroethane (DDT) to control mosquitoes and other biting insects that lived in the swamps and marshes along Florida's beaches and in the interior. Although first synthesized in 1874, the application of this pesticide as a method of controlling insects was discovered in 1939. By 1945, DDT was in common use, and "mosquito control" boards in all counties and municipalities sprayed generous amounts into the environment on a regular basis. While DDT did not kill all of the biting bugs, it did weaken their populations to such an extent that they no longer presented obstacles to developing new subdivisions. Rachel Carson's *Silent Spring*, published in 1962, questioned the indiscriminate use of pesticides, examining its effects on both the environment and humans, and in 1972, DDT was banned in the United States. Although its long-term effects included severe damage to the ecology of the Sunshine State, its short-term use made the state more habitable for humans.

Air conditioning, which had its origins with Dr. John Gorrie in Apalachicola, Florida, in 1851, had gradually evolved as a viable way to control heat and humidity in buildings. First used in factories, theatres and department stores, cooling systems were adapted to passenger cars on railroads and even automobiles by the 1930s. Willis Haviland Carrier experimented with air conditioning for homes as well, and by 1929, he had managed to create a system that was easily installed and maintained. The onslaught of the Great Depression prevented its widespread adoption by American homeowners, but here and there, air conditioning was added to existing homes. The first residential system in Florida was installed in Cocoa in 1935 when architect Richard Rummell touted the benefits of a York system as a palliative for the chronic bronchitis suffered by his client's son, John V. D'Albora. Within ten years after the end of the war, window air conditioning units, developed by the De La Vergne Company in 1935, became staples in most new homes in Florida, and even older homes were equipped with them as well. By the mid-1960s, central air systems were demanded by home purchasers. The highly negative publicity about hot summers in the Sunshine State bowed to the power of refrigerated air and no longer shaped the travel plans of tourists. For the first time in its history, the Sunshine State offered a year-round vacation experience.

Jet planes and pressurized cabins were also products of World War II innovation, and with the introduction of the de Havilland Comet in 1949, air travel became the most popular way to reach Florida. The Boeing Corporation soon followed this British innovation with its "Dash 80" model and the more popular 707. Throughout the Sunshine State, cities converted the long runways of abandoned military installations to jet travel and settled in to wait for the hordes of tourists they were sure would follow. Cities with no airport quickly began the construction of one.

In 1950, Florida's population exceeded two million residents for the first time and approached the three million mark. Between 1940 and 1980, increasing numbers of older people came to the state, leading some pundits to remark on "the graying of Florida." In 1940, 6.9 percent of the population was sixty-five and older, and by 1980, that figure had reached 17.3 percent. Warm weather twelve months a year, portable pensions and Social Security checks, no state income tax and a plethora of unfinished subdivisions provided the main attractions to lure them south. Some cities catered to the senior citizens. St. Petersburg became a mecca for them, and the main streets of the city were lined with the famous "green benches" where thousands met daily to talk with friends or simply to watch the activities on the street. Small hotels and boardinghouses, previously patronized by seasonal tourists, were overrun by seniors. One wag referred to the city as "a great lobby where people went to wait for death." In the short run, older new residents provided a boon to local hotel owners, but gradually government authorities realized that this was more than offset by growing demands for city services—fire, medical, transportation—and by increases in welfare programs needed to stretch static incomes. Miami Beach became a favorite retirement venue for thousands of northerners, particularly Jews, and by 1960, the city built by Carl Fisher was 80 percent Jewish. By the early 1970s, civic leaders tried to dispel the idea of Florida as a haven for the elderly. St. Petersburg removed its green benches, and Miami Beach was reclaimed by society's trendsetters.

The postwar explosion in Florida's population soon attracted individuals and companies eager to exploit the market they created for housing. Arthur Vining Davis, the founder of the Aluminum Company of America (ALCOA), sensed opportunity in the Sunshine State. In 1948, he left Pittsburgh and settled in Miami, bringing his massive fortune with him. Through the Arvida Corporation (ARthur VIning DAvis), his real estate company, he began to invest heavily in raw land and in the purchase of several landmarks of the Florida boom. In 1956, he paid $22.5 million for Addison Mizner's Boca Raton Hotel and Club and $13.5 million for Sarasota's Ringling Isles. Much like his predecessor in Miami, George Merrick, he envisioned the creation of complete towns with shopping districts, schools, churches, banks and government buildings, all financed, built and serviced by the Arvida Corporation or one of its subsidiaries. When Arvida stock was offered on the market, it was instantly sold out—just in time for the collapse of 1959.

The Mackle brothers—Elliot, Robert and Frank Jr.—created the General Development Corporation in 1954 with assets of about $125 million. They bought huge swaths of undeveloped land and immediately began the process of transforming raw acreage into cities. Port Malabar (now Palm Bay, the largest city in Brevard County), Port St. Lucie (the largest city in St. Lucie County), Key Biscayne, Port St. John, North Port, Deltona and Sebastian Highlands were carved out of pasture and wetlands, but Port Charlotte on the west coast was their masterpiece. Designed to encompass more land and houses than Detroit, the company spent millions turning scrubland into neatly sectioned blocks.

The success of the General Development Corporation generated a great deal of competition. Coral Ridge Properties, Del Webb, Gulf American Land

Company and several other development companies entered the market. Some of these companies, like the Gulf American Land Company owned by Jack and Leonard Rosen, dealt primarily in raw land sales, which they marketed through radio, television, newspapers and magazine campaigns. These rivaled the earlier campaigns of Fisher and Merrick in Miami. Others built modestly priced bungalows aimed at capturing the growing number of middle-class buyers. Utilizing the "a little down, small monthly payments" approach to sell their property, promoters realized astronomical profits. Jim Walters took to the airwaves and used Jim and Jesse McReynolds and the Virginia Boys, a bluegrass band, to promote his shell homes. The Jim Walters Corporation would put in the foundation and erect the exterior and roof of the home; the interior was left for the buyer to finish. "A dollar and a deed is all you need" went the slogan, and it brought in millions for the company.

The Sunshine State was in the midst of another boom, and 3,000 new residents each week gave credence to the claims of promoters that this one would last. When Florida promoters took their companies to Wall Street, they became the hottest-selling stocks in the market. Values doubled, then tripled and even quadrupled as investors clamored to be part of the boom. Florida's population, which had been 2,771,000 in 1950, reached 4,951,000. All of these new residents needed a place to live, didn't they? Then, disaster struck.

The U.S. economy went into a mild recession in 1959, and many of those who had purchased land or homes on the installment plan could not continue to make the small monthly payments and walked away from their purchases. The rate of foreclosures shot up. Promoters, like their counterparts in the 1920s, had counted these long-term contracts when valuing their companies and now faced ruin when subcontractors demanded payment for work on their developments.

To add to the misery of the land promoters, the rainy season that year was one of the wettest on record. For sixty consecutive days and nights, it rained incessantly. Hastily cleared land, even acreage with new drainage canals in place, flooded. It really didn't matter that a property was in a one-hundred-year flood plain; the reality was that 1959 was a flood year and there was no guarantee that 1960 would not be a repeat performance. Nature operated on its own schedule, not according to some arbitrary calendar imposed by man. Another bust?

Perhaps—however, not as bad as that of 1927. On May 25, 1961, President John F. Kennedy, in a speech to Congress, delivered some relief when he said:

I believe this Nation should commit itself to achieving the goal, before this decade is out, of landing a man on the moon and returning him safely to earth. No single space project in this period will be more impressive to mankind, or more important for the long-range exploration of space; and none will be so difficult or expensive to accomplish.

The race for space was on, and Florida was the immediate beneficiary.

At Cape Canaveral, the National Aeronautics and Space Administration, which had been created in 1958, was the recipient of massive funding from Congress and immediately put out the call for engineers and workers of all kinds. Rural Brevard County, which had been in the backwater of previous developments, now found itself overwhelmed by the thousands who answered the call. Housing was in such small supply that engineers with doctorates were forced to sleep in culverts and concrete pipes alongside the roads that were being built to connect the space center with the mainland. Anyone with an extra room in their house was urged to rent it to a space worker. Garages, barns and unused outbuildings were quickly occupied. Contractors from all over the nation rushed to Brevard County to build houses for the families of the newcomers, and local governments rushed to build the infrastructure that was needed to service the Cape. The hullaballoo was even greater than Miami had experienced in 1925.

Cocoa Beach, a 1920s development of Gus Edwards, had lain fallow for forty years. Few houses dotted the barrier island for several decades, but suddenly its proximity to the space center pushed sales toward the sky. Motels, restaurants, houses and apartment buildings rose from the marshes and barren sands overnight. Cocoa, Titusville and Cocoa Beach became gold-rush towns as eager thousands, pointed straight to the space center by the old Dixie Highway, came to find work. Bust? Maybe on the west coast of Florida, but not here. By 1965, the need for housing had been met and exceeded, and the Space Coast bubble burst. Not to worry, there was another bubble coming.

In Florida, desirable beach properties were becoming scarce. Faced with this growing shortage, developers turned to finding new ways to maximize what was left. The answer was simple—condominiums. Instead of dedicating a half acre or acre to a single home, promoters discovered that they could take that same piece of property and build vertically to create residences for more people. Looking much like apartment buildings, condominiums offered much more to builders. Gone were the hassles of dealing with temporary renters and the need for constant maintenance. Under the generous laws passed by the Florida legislature, condominiums are made up of individually owned units that can be bought and sold as such. Governed by an association of owners, purchasers were assessed monthly fees for maintenance and larger assessments for repairs. The 1961 Housing Act allowed the Federal Housing Administration to insure mortgages on condominium units, and the availability of funding touched off another boom. Although condominiums made their first appearance on the crowded beaches of the Miami area, they soon spread throughout the Sunshine State. Soon, the other forty-nine states and much of the industrialized world boasted "condo canyons," which were praised as answers to urban sprawl and the demand for more urban dwellings.

In Florida, condominiums appealed to retirees who wanted to escape the maintenance problems that individual homes presented and who wanted to spend the last years of their lives free of such burdens. Even the emergence of "condo Nazis," unit owners serving on condo association boards who enforced rigid rules governing what could and could not be done by individual owners, did not halt the condominium explosion. Americans from other states were particularly attracted to buying condominiums in the Sunshine State. An amendment to the state's constitution, passed at the height of the boom of the 1920s, prohibited the imposition of a state income tax. The end result was the growth of buyers who, after six months and a day, declared their condominium their permanent residence, registered to vote and moved their assets to Florida. Many of these new residents retained their homes in other states and only visited Florida seasonally after they had established residency. Condominiums were the new Coral Gables or Boca Raton. Happy days were here again!

Real Estate Investment Trusts (REITs), first created in 1960, added to the condominium boom. Established strictly to aid investors, the primary benefit is that REITs are subject to no or low corporate income taxes as long as 90 percent of their income is distributed to investors, private or public. REITs became the instrument of choice for new developments since individual investments in a single project could be minimized and additional funds invested in a number of projects. The risks were minimized as well since the failure of one project did not usually mean a loss of all investments.

In 1958, rumors began circulating that something big was going to happen in the Orlando area. What it was exactly, few people knew, and they were not talking. Slowly, anonymous buyers started to purchase large and small plots of citrus land and pasture, accumulating some twenty-seven thousand acres. Eventually, the news leaked that Walt Disney was the money behind the purchases, and Florida would become the home of Disney World, a new and expanded version of Disney Land in California. The legislature of Florida was so impressed that in 1967 it voted to give the Walt Disney Company unprecedented governmental powers—not as an incorporated city that might be subject to the whims of future legislators but as an independent agency with powers that exceeded those of a normal corporation. It was exempt from state and local zoning laws, which meant that the company could build anything it wanted on its property (including a nuclear power plant) without fear of any regulation from county or state entities. In addition, it could offer tax-free municipal bonds to raise money for future development. Most importantly, the Disney Company gained the right to annex adjoining property through eminent domain, a power usually reserved for elected governments.

Disney World opened on October 1, 1971, to instant success. More than eleven million visitors came the first year of operation, and the numbers continued to grow during the second and third years. Originally, the Disney Company projected four thousand employees, but that figure was doubled immediately and had doubled again by 1973. Surrounding the theme park, hundreds of lesser attractions and scores of new hotels opened to accommodate visitors. Orlando, which had never had a significant tourist industry before, suddenly became the destination of choice of many Americans, and the boom generated new businesses throughout central Florida. Yeah, Florida had sold its soul to the Mouse, but look at what it got in return!

The first hint of trouble came not from Florida but from the small oil-producing countries of the Middle East. By the beginning of the 1970s, world gold prices had reached $800 an ounce, and in 1971, President Richard Nixon ended America's policy of backing its currency with gold at a rate of $35 an ounce. Oil prices were pegged to the U.S. dollar and had not changed significantly since the end of World War II. The situation needed to be addressed, and quickly. For oil-producing countries, the opportunity to do so came quickly. The United States had resupplied the Israeli military at the end of the Yom Kippur War in 1973, much to the displeasure of Arab countries. In retaliation for the United States' support of Israel, OPEC, the Organization of Arab Petroleum Exporting Countries, imposed an embargo on oil shipments to the United States until an acceptable peace deal had been worked out between Israel and its neighbors. When the embargo ended in 1974, higher prices for crude oil had been established. The problems created by the embargo were exacerbated by the tremendous expenditures of the

U.S. government in fighting the Vietnam War. At the same time, federal spending on the War on Poverty poured more money into the economy. The overall economy faced additional problems as prices for manufactured goods rose and salaries remained the same—stagnation.

The oil embargo produced repercussions in every level of American society and seriously affected the Sunshine State. At the gas pumps, prices rose to previously unseen prices but were brought down to an acceptable level when Nixon imposed wage and price controls. Tourism, which was based on automobile and airplane travel, slackened as Americans curtailed their driving and airlines raised prices to compensate for higher fuel prices. In Orlando, Disney announced the termination of two thousand workers. If the Mouse was cutting back, so should everyone else.

The wage and price freezes of the Nixon administration proved to be disastrous, and Gerald Ford, the new interim president, seemed incapable of dealing with the situation. He left a muddled economy for his successor, Jimmy Carter, to deal with. Carter, too, was incapable of doing so. A second oil embargo, precipitated by the Iranian Revolution in 1979, added to the economic woes of the United States. Long lines at service stations were the order of the day as Americans sought to fill their tanks with this necessary commodity, which was now in short supply. Once again, prices rose on petroleum-based manufactured items.

Fixed interest rates for new homes, which had hovered around 5.5 percent annually, suddenly rose to 7.5 percent and higher. Payments on adjustable rate mortgages (ARMs), which were pegged to the prime rate of interest and had been introduced as a way to allow marginally qualified buyers into the residential market, skyrocketed. Homeowners found themselves unable to meet the higher monthly payments as salaries remained the same and the cost of other consumer goods rose. Foreclosure signs appeared in virtually every neighborhood.

REITs found the going tough, too. Huge condominium and apartment complexes found no buyers, and investors faced the possibility of losing everything. Some sought to convert their unfilled complexes with temporary residents by selling two-week residencies as "time shares." If buyers couldn't afford to own a condo outright, they could settle for two weeks each year in some exotic development. For a one-time purchase price and annual maintenance fees, the buyer could claim partial ownership in a condo. Not a perfect solution, but one that worked in the short term.

Savings and loan associations, usually regarded as the most conservative financial institutions in the nation, invested heavily in the real estate market of the late 1960s and early 1970s. As the economic slump continued during the decade, the financial toll of these investments pushed these institutions to the wall. By the beginning of the 1980s, the nation faced its first potential bank failure crisis as more and more of the thrifts (and some banks as well) had to call on the federal government to bail them out. The Federal Savings and Loan Insurance Corporation was called on to replace depositor funds lost in real estate speculation. Major borrowers, unable to meet the payments on loans, simply walked away, leaving the institutions with empty finished buildings or buildings still under construction.

John Ellis "Jeb" Bush, son of one U.S. president, brother to another and a two-term governor of the Sunshine State, was one such borrower. He defaulted on a $4.5 million loan in Miami, eventually settling his debt for $500,000 and leaving taxpayers to pay the remainder. Another brother, Neil, was director of the Silverado Savings and Loan in Denver, which failed, eventually costing taxpayers $1.3 billion. The U.S. Office of Thrift Supervision investigated Silverado's failure and determined that Bush had engaged in numerous "breaches of his fiduciary duties involving multiple conflicts of interest" but failed to file criminal charges. He paid $50,000 to settle a civil suit brought against him. The entire crisis cost the American taxpayers $150 billion to resolve.

Although costing them enormous amounts in tax dollars, Americans were blasé about the savings and loan's failures, perhaps because the full extent of the crisis played out over the entire decade of the '80s; perhaps because they were tired of bad economic news; perhaps because of the stature of the people involved; or perhaps because the conclusion of the crisis faded into obscurity when the United States got involved in a new war in the Middle East. Perhaps.

During the decade of the '90s, the American economy gradually recovered. The real estate market took a backseat to the ".com" boom that was centered in California. Enormous sums of venture capital, which might have normally gone into real estate, were poured instead into startup companies and exotic web-based operations that marketed everything from social contacts to banking, from the contents of entire specialty stores to airline tickets, from video games to…real estate? The expansion of the Internet changed American commerce forever, and no new company, nor one that had been in business for decades, could afford to compete without a website or shopping cart. The world joined in. The outsourcing of critical services to underdeveloped countries became the bane of the consumer's existence as he tried to understand "Steve," whose accent was neither American nor British but sounded suspiciously like Hindi or Pashtu. Even government agencies outsourced critical functions to nameless, faceless voices in foreign countries or to private industry in the United States. It was, pundits alleged, simply the realities of a global marketplace. The ".com" bubble, like most bubbles, soon burst. By 2000, most of the startup companies had either succeeded wildly or were gone from the scene.

The new century started on a high note for the United States and for Florida. It combined two of the twentieth century's biggest bubbles into one. Stocks climbed to record highs as the federal government, followed closely by state governments, adopted a pro-business stance and passed numerous pieces of legislation designed to aid investors. Estate taxes were reduced, and the amount of an estate exempted from "death taxes" was raised. Burdensome laws, many of them left over from the New Deal, were repealed or watered down. Banks were allowed to engage in speculative activities, and brokers were allowed to create new instruments for investment. Loan standards, which had once focused on annual income and debt levels, went out the window. Subprime mortgages, guaranteed by government agencies, were offered to virtually anyone. Indeed, lending institutions were required by law to allocate a percentage of the loans they made to individuals who could not qualify for a traditional loan. Government grants provided down payments in some cases, and mortgage assistance was available to lower monthly payments. Money was so plentiful that simply filling out a loan application was often enough to secure a loan of some kind. Step up and sign on the dotted line!

Mailboxes were indiscriminately flooded with letters guaranteeing recipients "pre-approved" loans without cumbersome or restrictive credit checks. Online mortgage companies followed suit, clogging the Internet with unsolicited offers to lend money. Adjustable rate mortgages, the scourge of the 1970s, made a reappearance. Lenders who could not even come up with a small down payment on a new home were offered multiple loans to cover down payments, closing costs and other incidental expenses. Gone were the days when a borrower might deal face-to-face with his banker and find a sympathetic friend in tough times. Instead, borrowers saw a lender briefly at the start of the loan process, and that was the only time. Loans, once made, were "bundled" together and sold to investors who then traded the bundles on the stock market. Investors in newly emerging nations—China, Korea, Taiwan—and the oil-rich sheikdoms of the Middle East eagerly snapped these up. Even the federal government, engaged in two wars, got in the act, selling bonds and treasury bills by the billions to overseas investors at unprecedented levels.

In Florida, condominium sales, which had faltered in the wake of the savings and loan crisis, were suddenly rejuvenated as Americans poured their profits from a constantly rising stock market into purchasing them. Sales were so strong that many investors sold their homes or mortgaged them to the hilt to put down payments on unfinished units at preconstruction prices and "flip" them for higher prices when the project was finished. It was not unusual for a single investor to purchase three or four units in the same building. With a mere $100,000, an investor could control property worth millions. For many, the profits to be made would be their retirement fund. What could go wrong?

"Flipping" entered the American lexicon as a noun. In the residential home market, flipping became the new "ostrich farm" or "emu ranch." It was a quick way to make a fortune. All you had to do was buy a run-down property, invest "sweat equity" or a little money to fix it up and put it back on the market at a higher price. Television shows chronicling the adventures of "flippers" received some of the highest ratings each season. Get-rich gurus, filmed surrounded by the toys of success, touted "systems" to wannabe millionaires guaranteeing them that they could buy properties with nothing down and sell them for enormous profits. It was foolproof.

In Florida, the years from the 1980s to the beginning of the first decade of the twenty-first century saw a return of the "planned" community concept. In 1979, in isolated Walton County in the Panhandle, which had no zoning or building codes, builder/developer Robert Davis introduced his "New Urbanist" Seaside development to the world. Sounding strangely like George Merrick's City Beautiful in Coral Gables, it features a strict building code that governs the exteriors of all buildings and other architectural elements, as well as standards on the size of lots. In Brevard County, the Viera Company, an offshoot of the A. Duda and Sons agricultural empire, began construction on its Viera planned community in 1993. Located in former cow pastures, the development extends for several miles on both sides of I-95. In addition to schools, churches and homes, Viera also has several commercial centers, including the Avenue, an outdoor mall featuring high-end stores. The Duda Company offers one-stop shopping for homebuyers, and its subsidiaries include Viera Realty, which handles sales, and Viera Builders, which constructs the homes in the development. In the Kissimmee-Orlando area, the Disney Company developed its Celebration community in 1996 and announced plans for additional communities. Like Seaside and Viera, Celebration is governed by strictly enforced architectural and building codes.

Something happened to the latest boom in 2007–08. The nation's financial institutions suddenly discovered that they were over invested in mortgage bundles and that the market for them had maxed out. This discovery led to a major collapse of banks, now numbering in excess of two hundred and predicted to rise to as many as four hundred before the crisis is over. Another four hundred banks have been placed on the FDIC's "problem list." The cause? Too many "toxic" subprime real estate loans.

Major brokerage houses and other large institutions are in trouble today (2009) because of investments in the same loans, which precipitated a severe decline in stock market values (approximately 40 percent of all stocks) and a corresponding decline in home values. Individuals who had purchased homes and condos to flip found their values to be significantly lower than what they had paid for them. One by one, they lost them or gave up their investments when no new buyers stepped forward to purchase them. The dreams of a comfortable retirement built on real estate profits vanished. Some of the investors, having placed their entire estate in such purchases, were forced back into the labor pool.

New owners, particularly those with ARMs, discovered that they were "upside down" as residential values dropped below the face value of the mortgages. When they attempted to renegotiate their mortgages with lending institutions, most discovered that to be impossible since they had been bundled with other mortgages and sold and resold many times. Who now held them was virtually impossible to discover. Lending institutions that had made subprime mortgages were left with abandoned pieces of property as homeowners abandoned loans that they could never repay. These "toxic" assets skewed the balance sheets of banks and savings and loan companies to the negative side. Lending practically ceased, and all real estate sales ground to a halt. The federal government announced the creation of its "Making Home Affordable" plan in March 2009, committing $50 billion to homeowners and mortgage companies for loan modifications. Some 360,000 homeowners and forty-eight mortgage companies signed up to participate in the first three months of the program. The million homeowners across the United States are eligible for assistance.

Companies did not escape the crash of 2007–08. The credit they depended on dried up. The automobile industry suffered a double hit as gasoline prices rose to 1979 levels and buyers could not be found for the low mileage, highly polluting cars Detroit manufactured. Foreign automobile manufacturers, more technologically advanced, offered hybrids that were partially powered by electrical motors and delivered more miles-per-gallon and lower rates of carbon dioxide emissions. In desperation, two of the "Big Three" manufacturers, General Motors and Chrysler, approached the federal government for bailout money. The difficulties the auto manufacturers faced were similar to those faced in all other industries. Consumers weren't buying, companies were losing money, layoffs and downsizing were the order of the day—all of which triggered another spiral. Soon companies in all areas began to agitate for bailout money.

The American economy was in a tailspin. It was 1929 all over again, but with major differences. Unlike the Hoover administration, today's political leaders appear determined to move quickly to avoid further damage to the economy. In the final three months of his tenure, President George W. Bush, reacting to predictions of a financial meltdown that would extend to the world's markets, engineered the $700 billion Toxic Asset Recovery Program bailout financed by American taxpayers. His successor, Barack Obama, accepted the Bush plan as his own and pushed to implement it. The TARProgram was a public relations disaster from the beginning, particularly after dying banks paid employees huge bonuses for having sold the very assets that caused the crisis in the first place, and taxpayers reacted loudly. The program remained in place, and only a few banks opted to eschew the money in favor of staff bonuses.

The automobile manufacturers, who came by private jet to Washington, also stirred up a hornet's nest of public outrage. Taxpayers, who had less to lose if the automobile industry collapsed, reacted to this display of ostentatious spending—especially when the CEOs were begging hat-in-hand for relief—with tremendous anger. Although Congress demanded serious corporate reform and downsizing as conditions for assistance, it agreed to make $25 billion available in loans to the corporations. Better than 1929, when there was no bailout!

At this writing (September 2009), the collapse of 2007–08 has been mitigated somewhat as the bailouts by the federal government—and those of other governments around the world—take hold, but even now the future is uncertain. In Florida, home sales are on the rise, but more than two-thirds of all sales are short sales as financial institutions liquidate their toxic assets. Homeowners who have managed to hang on find themselves with property that has been devalued by about 40 percent yet face increased taxes as governments raise levies to compensate for decreased values. Governments, struggling to pay for infrastructure improvements and services contracted for in the boom three years ago, try to downsize personnel and limit spending. Unemployment figures rise monthly, and the conventional wisdom is to accept the fact that joblessness will continue to rise, but attention should be placed on how slowly it rises. Foreclosures are also on the rise, but once again, conventional wisdom stresses how slowly they increase.

Yet, there is a glimmer of defiance and hope. There are believers. The Miami Corporation, a corporate entity of the Deering family holdings, recently announced that it was converting a large part of its ninety-four-square-mile Farmton Tree Farm property in Brevard and Volusia Counties into residential sites. Under a fifty-year plan, the first twenty-three hundred homes will be in Brevard County, along with two million square feet of commercial, manufacturing, professional and retail space. The Viera Company, apparently unfazed by the depression economy, added its voice to the ranks of the optimists when it announced the construction of fourteen hundred new units in Viera. However, a quick reminder is in order. George E. Merrick, faced with falling sales for his Coral Gables development, announced the $250 million South Seas Islands of Coral Gables just a few months before he went bankrupt. He, too, was a believer.

For the first time in its history, more people left Florida in 2008 than took up residence. Perhaps historian Gary R. Mormino hit the nail on the head in an interview in August 2009 when he referred to the state as a Ponzi scheme. "Since the 1950s, Florida has been attracting about a thousand people every single day, 85 million tourists last year. Our entire structure, our tax structure, is built upon growth," he said.

> And the mantra has always been, "growth will pay for itself." No one ever really, I think, gave serious attention to the fact [of] what will happen when a thousand people stop coming? And, that's what I meant by the Ponzi scheme, that yesterday's homeowners will pay for today's newcomers. And, the newcomers stopped coming about two years ago.

Is it really over?

A Brief Note on Sources

The boom of the 1920s is one of the most written-about subjects in Florida history. Most of the books and articles about the boom are localized in their focus and fail to deal with the entire state, but all of them are wonderful sources of information. Works by Paul S. George, Arva Moore Parks, Donn Curl, Stuart McIver, Gene Burnett, Theodore Van Itallie, Lindsay Williams, Hampton Dunn, Jerrell Shofner, Charles E. Harner and others provide invaluable information culled from interviews and the libraries of local historical societies. The growth of the Internet has produced a prodigious number of primary and secondary sources on events, locations and individuals who figured prominently in the period. Of particular interest to the researcher are two contemporary books that offer special insights into the "official" explanations of the boom and the later bust. Written in 1925, Frank Parker Stockbridge and John Holliday Perry's *Florida in the Making* (Kingsport, TN: Kingsport Press, 1926) offers nothing but assurances that the real estate boom will continue, while their *So This Is Florida* (Jacksonville, FL: J.H. Perry Publishing Company, 1938) says very little about the boom or bust. Interesting, to say the least. T.H. Weigall's *Boom in Paradise* (New York: Alfred H. King, 1932) offers a firsthand account of Miami in early 1926 and the George E. Merrick development of Coral Gables.

In 1984, the Harcourt, Brace, Jovanovich Company had the good sense to publish David Nolan's *Fifty Feet in Paradise: The Booming of Florida*, which is the best overall book about the boom and the following decades through the early 1980s. Gary Ross Mormino, a Tampa historian of the Florida experience, took up where Nolan left off and published *Land of Sunshine, State of Dreams: A Social History of Modern Florida* (Gainesville: University Press of Florida, 2005) to bring the story of Florida's development up to date. There have been many changes since 2005, and the Florida Mormino wrote about has morphed once again into something new. Hopefully, the next edition will include another chapter to keep *Land of Sunshine* current. Both Nolan and Mormino write in a conversational, flowing style that makes their books easy to read and appealing to the public. These two books are terrific—essential—primers for anyone interested in the social and economic history of Florida during the last three centuries.

Critical to understanding the complex financial deals that provided the credit necessary for development in the 1920s is Raymond B. Vickers's *Panic in Paradise: Florida's Banking Crash of 1926* (Tuscaloosa: University of Alabama Press, 1994). Vickers documents the unethical and illegal dealings of bankers and developers who controlled the state's financial institutions and the failure of federal and state regulators to stop the looting and pillaging of them. Vickers's book also makes it possible to understand some of the more recent financial misdeeds that sent the savings and loan institutions crashing in the 1980s and the banks and investment firms in 2007–08. The old adage that there is nothing new under the sun certainly applies to financial institutions.

Several biographies provide excellent sources of information and insights into the personalities of boomers. Mark S. Foster's *Castles in the Sand: The Life and Times of Carl Graham Fisher* (Gainesville: University Press of Florida, 2000) is invaluable in understanding the creation of Miami Beach. Less valuable but still useful is Polly Redford's *Billion-Dollar Sandbar: A Biography of Miami Beach* (New York: E.P. Dutton & Co., Inc., 1970). Practically useless from a factual standpoint but filled with anecdotes is Alva Johnston's *The Legendary Mizners* (New York: American Book/Stratford Press, Inc., 1942). Johnston was infatuated with the life and lifestyle of Wilson Mizner, Addison's younger brother, and his book is primarily an encomium to him. Michael J. Boonstra's thesis, "D.P. Davis and the Florida Land Boom" (master's thesis, California State University Dominguez Hills, 2002), is a good start in exploring the life of this legendary developer. The life of George E. Merrick is covered in Kathryne Belden Ashley's out-of-print *George E. Merrick and Coral Gables, Florida* (Coral Gables, FL: Crystal Bay Publishers, 1985). Glenn Hammond Curtiss's life is covered in Cecil R. Roseberry's *Glenn Curtiss, Pioneer of Flight* (Syracuse, NY: Syracuse University Press, 1991). David C. Weeks authored the definitive biography of John Ringling in *Ringling: The Florida Years, 1911–1936* (Gainesville: University Press of Florida, 1993).

Robert E. Snyder and Jack B. Moore offer a great deal of information, both textually and in pictures, in their *Pioneer Commercial Photography: The Burgert Brothers, Tampa, Florida* (Cocoa: Florida Historical Society Press, 2007). Donn Curl and the Boca Raton Historical Society recently published a pictorial history of Addison Mizner's prized Boca Raton Inn, *The Boca Raton Resort & Club: Mizner's Inn* (Charleston, SC: The History Press, 2008), which provides a good look at the architecture and operation of the Mizner Development Corporation.

The role of golf in the explosion of development in the 1920s is explored in Richard Moorhead and Nick Wynne's pictorial history *Golf in Florida, 1886–1950* (Charleston, SC: Arcadia Publishing, 2009). An expanded text-driven book is scheduled for publication at a later date. The Moorhead Collection of historical pictures and postcards is large and growing.

Florida is blessed with a number of photographic and documentary archives. The Florida Historical Society Library in Cocoa has an extensive postcard collection, which covers the 1920s. In addition, it has a number of original advertisements for the period and a collection of period magazines, including *American Motorist*. The Florida Historical Society Library is also home to the Mosquito Beaters, a community reunion organization with Florida photographs dating back to the 1880s. The Mosquito Beaters, particularly Grand Sachem George Leland "Speedy" Harrell, are a wonderful source of firsthand accounts of Sunshine State developments from the 1920s to the present.

The Historical Association of Southern Florida in Miami, which counts George E. Merrick as one of its founders, also possesses a marvelous archive of period photographs and other materials. So, too, does the Florida Photographic Archives in Tallahassee. The Tampa-Hillsborough County Library System holds the bulk of the Burgert Brothers Photograph Collection, while the Special Collections Department of the University of South Florida Library also has a significant number of Burgert Brothers photographs in its Hampton Dunn Collection.

These are merely starting points for any researcher on the 1920s or real estate development in the Sunshine State. We are deeply indebted to them all.

About the Authors

Nick Wynne is executive director emeritus of the Florida Historical Society. He obtained his PhD in history from the University of Georgia (1980) and taught at several southern universities. He has published seven books on Florida history, many of them with Arcadia Publishing, including *Tin Can Tourists of Florida, Florida in the Civil War, Florida's Antebellum Homes* and *Golf in Florida, 1886–1950*. In addition, he has won several awards for his books, including the James J. Horgan Award for Best Florida Fiction for Juveniles. He is also the author of a forthcoming novel, *Pirkle Hall or Sister Mary Magdalene and the Church of the Archangel Rodney*. He and his coauthor, Richard Moorhead, are proud graduates of Telfair County High School in McRae, Georgia—class of 1961.

Richard Moorhead is a retired sales executive with the Ethicon, Inc. division of Johnson and Johnson. He currently is president/CEO of Richard Moorhead Associates, LLC, a medical sales, sales management and marketing executive search firm. A graduate of Valdosta State University and Webster University, he lives with his wife, Sandy, in Winter Park. An avid golfer, he is the coauthor of *Golf in Florida, 1886–1950*. Along with Nick Wynne, he is the coauthor of *Floating Fortress: Florida in World War II*, which will be published by The History Press in 2010.

Visit us at
www.historypress.net